DATE DUE

WHERE IS HOME?

LIVING THROUGH FOSTER CARE

E. P. JONES

AFTERWORD BY
DR. EDMUND GORDON
JOHN M. MUSSER PROFESSOR OF
PSYCHOLOGY, YALE UNIVERSITY

FOUR WALLS EIGHT WINDOWS
NEW YORK

First printing February, 1990.

While the institutions, events and places referred to in
Where Is Home? are real, the names of persons have all been changed.
Any resemblance to the names of persons living or dead is
a coincidence of which the author has no present knowledge.

Library of Congress Cataloging-in-Publication Data

Jones, E. P., 1958–
Where is home? : living through foster care / E. P. Jones ;
afterword by Edmund Gordon.
p.   cm.

0-941423-34-4 ISBN $17.95
1. Jones, E. P., 1958-   . 2. Foster children—New York (N.Y.)—
Biography.   3. Foster home care—New York (N.Y.)—Case studies.
I. Title.
HV885.N5J66   1989
362.7′33′097471—dc20   8939770
                                                       CIP

Four Walls Eight Windows
P.O. Box 548, Village Station
New York, N.Y. 10014

Designed by Cindy LaBreacht.
Printed in the U.S.A.

First Edition.

CONTENTS

ACKNOWLEDGMENTS

Many people have lent their support and long hours to make my dream a reality. To these individuals, who were so tolerant during my periods of despair, I am forever grateful for their patience and understanding: Dr. Edmund Gordon of Yale University, who wrote the Afterword; Christine and Jeff Quinn, who convinced me that my story was worth writing down in the first place and then got me through the first draft; Marie Brown, who guided me through the intricacies of the book publishing world as my agent; Iva Loftman, who courageously typed the manuscript off of hand-written legal pads; Megan McLemore, the attorney who won my battle with the state of New York to have my records released so that I could include them in this book; A. J. Powell, who first described my story in the *New York Voice*; and Dan Simon, my editor, whose patience is an ever-enduring gift.

Each of you were there when it counted. To you, and to foster care children everywhere, who are my inspiration: May your light shine through.

—E. P. JONES
JANUARY 1990

SUMMARY OF PLACEMENT*

RE: PAMELA JONES   D.O.B. 8/21/58

Pamela is the oldest of two children born to Frank
Jones and Elizabeth Cunningham. She was born
8/21/58. Mrs. Jones deserted the family when
Pam was four years old. The father remarried and
the new wife refused to take Pam. Pam was then
placed in Callagy Hall at the age of six. From
there Pam was involved in a series of placements
in foster homes and state hospitals most of which
were terminated by factors outside of Pam herself.

There is little known of Pam's early years. Her
maternal aunt, Mrs. Wittaker, reports that Pam's
mother, Mrs. Jones, was an alcoholic who found it
next to impossible to properly care for the children. Mrs. Wittaker reports that she would try to
care for the children, but this was very difficult
since Mrs. Jones exhibited paranoid tendencies

---

*St. Michael's Summary of Placement, Social Worker
notes, 9/21/73.

and would accuse her sister of trying to steal her children. Mrs. Wittaker said that Pam's early years were not normal. Her mother could not cope and her father did not care. Her mother's absconding was a severe rejection and not more than two years later Pam was again rejected by a maternal figure. Her memories of her father are that he promised to visit her at Callagy Hall and never did.

CHAPTER 1

DON'T BUILD BRIDGES

YOU CAN'T CROSS

Were I to draw my father from memory, he would appear to me as a silhouette, the outline of a figure of a man, and not the man himself. In my memory, he explains to me the process of tightening the skins of the bongoes that he had given me as a present. My mother stumbles around the room; I think she was laughing hysterically. My father turns to me and asks if I want to go out for a ride. Of course I do. No child turns down a ride. Leaving my mother behind, we jump in the car, arriving a short time later at a house not far from ours. Eager to go inside, I'm told to stay in the car and to be a good little girl. I scoot under the wheel, playing with the gears. The car begins to roll down the hill. Fortunately, my father is able to catch me before the car picks up speed.

This is the last time I can remember being with both parents. My mother deserted the family in 1962, when I was four, leaving me and my younger sister with my father. He was unable to find anyone else to take care of us. So in September 1964, I entered Callagy Hall, escorted by my father and one policeman. A lot of talking went on between the two of them.

"This is a shelter for children," the policeman said. I did not know that this would be my new home.

My father then said to me, "I'm going to leave you now."

I started to cry.

"Don't cry," he said, "I'll be back soon."

I recall awakening that night in a cold, dark hall. Sleeping cots were arranged in rows of six. The place reeked of urine. I could hear the sounds of mice scratching in the baseboards of the walls. I cried and whimpered all night, feeling alone and uncared for.

"Why me?" I asked myself over and over. "What did I do to deserve this?" No one could answer.

This continued for a week. After a while the crying stopped, but the feeling of loneliness increased. My father visited me one day. The smile it brought to my face! I thought he had come to take me home, but he'd only come to measure my finger for a little girl's ring. He promised to return; it's the kind of promise you hold on to. . . .

For thirteen years, life for me was being shifted from one agency to another, from foster homes to institutions, like a sack of potatoes.

I lived at Callagy Hall for two years before placement was found.

In June 1966, I vaguely remember entering my first foster home, somewhere in a middle-class neighborhood in Queens, New York. My stay would be brief. From what I can recall, the home was well-kept, with a nice yard, yet I'm left with faceless images of the guardians. I don't remember their names just the feeling of being terribly frightened by their drinking, loud voices, and beatings.

After a month of this, I tried to escape by running out of the house. A car nearly hit me. My foster mother came out yelling. She grabbed and beat me. The next day the social worker came to visit and I told her about the beatings.

"You're a liar," the social worker said, "and you'll have to leave," adding that she believed I had tried to commit suicide. She thought I was lying; I had not even begun to tell her the real truth. I was too scared to recount the incident of being fondled by a man who entered my room during a party given by the foster parents, and so I never told her all of what had taken place there. She waited while I packed my bags and then drove me to a summer camp. I wasn't yet eight years old, but my case record already counted three major rejections: first by my mother, then by my father and stepmother, and finally by my first foster mother. The loneliness just kept building inside.

Her foster mother of one month turned out to be a psychotic. After a camp placement, the family refused to take her back due to marital discord and no reason relating to Pam herself. Pam took this third rejection very badly. She underwent severe regression and depression.[1]

The social worker took me to a State facility in Rockland County. While driving there, she described the grounds, saying that there were plenty of trees and wide open fields. All I knew was that it was far away. How would my father know to visit me there? I asked myself over and over again. I didn't see much of the grounds because it was not how the social worker had described it. Rockland turned out to be a lock-up psychiatric facility.

One day, the Recreation department held a Maypole dance on the grounds for the residents. This was the only time I can recall being outside the building during my first three months. My room, like all the others, remained locked at night. Lying on my bed, I could hear the sounds of the doors slamming as they locked each one. With only the light of the moon shining through the barred window, I lay staring, wondering if anyone could hear the sounds of my sobbing. Eventually, I cried myself to sleep. That was the routine for me and as I think back, it must have been that way for all the others.

The feeling of having been branded by society as an outcast and an unwanted child stuck with me. But one nurse, Mrs. Jones, a tall, thin, African-American woman who worked the overnight shift, made me feel different. One night, when she heard me crying in my sleep during her midnight rounds, she entered my room to offer comfort. She sat down beside me and woke me from a nightmare as she asked, "What's wrong?"

"I want to go home."

"I know, soon."

We talked awhile about the things I liked—steak, ice cream and dolls. She promised that the next time she came on duty, she'd share some of her dinner with me. As I curled up, she said, "Come, let me get you a fresh pillowcase."

I wanted so much during these times to feel wanted and needed. Sometimes, when I felt lonely and depressed, I'd ask Mrs. Jones, "Can I go home with you?"

"I'm afraid not. It's against the rules," she'd say.

I didn't receive any visitors there, like some of the other children, at least none that I remember. But there was Mrs. Jones's special attention. I latched on to her like a lost puppy.

One night, after everyone else was asleep, she came to my room and unlocked the door. We headed down the hall to the kitchen, where I was her guest. I could smell the food before I reached the kitchen. I grinned from ear to ear with excitement. The meat was tender and filling, and I was hungry.

While serving the plates, she asked, "How was your day?"

"O.K., I guess," I responded, hunching my shoulders. "When can I go home? I don't like it here."

"I don't know," she answered.

After we ate and cleared the table, I went back to my room for the remainder of the night. Once again, I heard the key locking the door behind me. This night, though, had been better than all the rest; I had been able to enjoy a meal. This made me feel good, as only a forgotten child of eight could, if only for that moment. Soon I felt saddened by the sense of enclosure and the feeling of being shut out. I longed to return to my natural parents, to be in more familiar surroundings. Thoughts of home stayed on my mind. I remembered the rocking horse I once rode without a care in the world in the narrow, partially-lit hallway.

I kept away from the other children. Some had very severe problems: Down's syndrome, physical and mental disorders. I couldn't do anything about being there and it seemed no one else could either. One little girl was as thin as one could ever ask to be. We met while I was leaving the bathroom. She deliberately slammed the door on my pinky finger, breaking it to the point of permanent disfigurement. I wanted to wring her neck, but I couldn't. I was in excruciating pain as the blood flowed down my hand. It looked as though my finger had broken in two. Standing there, hysterically trying to figure out what this grey thing was hanging from my pinky, I screamed as loudly as I could. The attending nurse came running and escorted me to the nurses' station. As they bandaged, one of the nurses explained that the grey thing I was so upset about was my bone and that when exposed to air bone appears greyish in color. I sat shivering in tears. Through the glass casing I could see the girl snickering.

Everyone seemed crazy, in one way or another, except for Lori. She walked around with her thumb in her mouth. But she wasn't catatonic like so many of the others who rocked in their chairs, and she wasn't malicious. She seemed incapable of hurting another person intentionally. Lori seemed different.

Unlike my parents, Lori's would visit regularly. Some of the other residents' parents would at least visit during the holidays or leave gifts. I, on the other hand, received nothing.

Picture Lori as a large baby eleven years old, constantly whining and pestering the nurses for one thing or another. Lori appeared slow in her movements and thinking; by comparison with the others, she appeared harmless. When she couldn't bounce around the day room like a St. Bernard, she would sit in front of the T.V. and laugh, waiting until her parents would visit, bringing her candy and clothes. Every Saturday morning the attendants would wash her hair and dress her in her Sunday best. Afterwards, Lori would station herself at the door with her face pressed against the bars, waiting.

Except one day when Lori's parents cancelled their visit. The nurse on duty came to Lori with the news. Lori began to scream and stomp around, knocking over anything in her path including chairs and tables. Feeling her loneliness, I sat in a chair by the nurses' station, rocking and praying.

The nurse said, "Lori, if you continue, I'll have to give you a shot to calm you down!" Lori continued to vent her rage.

"Stop, Lori! Don't cry or the nurse will come," I warned. "Your parents will come next week. O.K.?"

Lori had tuned out. The nurse raced to the door to let the attendants in. They placed Lori on the floor, one holding her legs and the other placing the restraining jacket on in a tight fit.

"I'll behave! I won't do it anymore!" begged Lori.

"It's too late!" the nurse said. "Now you'll sit here."

After she calmed down, I went over and sat next to her on the couch.

"Your parents will come, you'll see. No one comes to see me."

"Why?"

"I don't know."

"Don't you have parents?"

"Yeah, I guess they don't care."

"When I go home, we go to the movies and sometimes horseback riding."

Listening to her, I became flushed with envy. I walked away, leaving Lori dozing off, talking to the T.V. My heart sank. I hadn't seen my mother or father for so long that I had forgotten what they looked like. I wondered just whom I resembled of the two and hated myself for thinking about it. My tears began to fall as I thought of it all and because I was unable to let them know how I felt; in silence, I pleaded for them to get me out of here.

I had been visiting the on-staff psychiatrist weekly for six months, starting one month after I had arrived here. At times, my feelings of despair would deepen, especially on holidays. I waited with each passing day for word on when I could return home, wondering whether Mommy and Daddy were still there. I would sit in one of the brightly colored chairs against the wall of the day room, close to the nurses' station, and drift into sad thoughts, unable to explain the desire I felt to be needed, bitterly thinking that I would never see home again, crying to return there. When asked by a nurse, "What's wrong?" all I could say was, "I want to go home." The nurse would answer, "I understand." How could anyone understand? They all had homes to go to and children of their own. I had no one.

Soon after the incident with my finger, a recommendation was made. The doctor diagnosed "depression" as the cause of my behavior but not "suicidal tendencies" as a social worker had stated earlier. Another social worker, this time from the Riverdale Agency for Children, was contacted, and was able to place me. I was eight and a half years old. Rockland County had held me within its walls for seven months. Upon release, I

was to go to a foster home in a middle-class neighborhood in Queens.

When we pulled up, on March 16, 1967, I stood for a
spell, stretching from the long drive down, looking
around, wondering which house it was on the block, as
the social worker gathered what few things I had from
the car. I asked myself what the foster parents would be
like and if they would want me. The social worker then
took my hand and said, "This is a nice family. You
should do well here!"

I noticed the dull grey and red of the house. As we
entered the gate, Mrs. Jackson greeted us from the door.
Once inside, the social worker and Mrs. Jackson sat in the
alcove. I stood by and listened. The social worker did
most of the talking. My thoughts began to drift away
from their conversation. Looking around, I thought, at
least the house is clean. I guess maybe it'll be O.K. here! I
won't have to be locked up in my room at night.

My new foster parents, the Jacksons, also cared for
another girl, Linda, a foster child placed by the same
agency placing me. Linda was fifteen, six and a half
years older than me. She wasn't home when I arrived.
After the social worker left, Mrs. Jackson showed me to
the room that I was to share with Linda and explained
where to put my clothes. She went on to tell me where
I'd be going to school. Assuming a meaningful air, she
said she knew the last family I was placed with. Since I
had already forgotten the faces of the last family, and

even the location of their house, I just looked at her with a blank expression.

A week or so later, I was enrolled in the nearby public school, entering the third grade. Being in a new school was frightening and I don't think it helped coming in right at the end of the school year. When I reached the doorway of the classroom, the teacher introduced me to the class and assigned me a desk. I sat listening to the others answer the questions the teacher gave as she called each out by name. When she got to me I couldn't answer the question and the other children began to laugh, while the girl seated behind me began to pull my hair. I jumped up, crying, and stormed out of the class.

School was very different from what I had expected it to be. I cannot recall whether I had attended classes at Rockland County. In any event, I had fallen behind for my age. I experienced a large adjustment problem due to the sense of distance I felt between myself and the other children. They would tease me about being chubby and having no mother or father. When I told the teacher, she did nothing to stop it. Not knowing what else to do, I would frequently walk out of the class just to escape the bullying.

Mrs. Jackson happened to be a crossing guard at the school. I quickly became acquainted with Mrs. Jackson's form of discipline. Each time she received a call from school about my walking out, I was sent to bed without dinner. This went on for some time. The more she punished me, the more defiant I became.

Ironically, Mrs. Jackson belonged to a sanctified Christian church. The congregation was lively and sang spirituals. The pastor never knew when to quit! At first, I didn't know what to think of it, people falling all over the place, dancing and crying to the beat of tambourines, shouting "Praise Him!"

Squirming in my seat with a childish grin that first Sunday, another little girl seated next to me offered me some gum. My smacking the gum caught the attention of Mrs. Jackson, seated in the choir loft. She motioned to the usher in the aisle to have me spit the gum out and I did. When service was over, I felt relieved that I didn't get hit. Willing and ready to go home, I grabbed my coat and headed for the door.

"Where you are going?" Mrs. Jackson asked.

"Aren't we going home?"

"Get over here and set the table! We're eating dinner here!"

We stayed in church all day every Sunday, until it seemed as though we'd never leave.

Then gospel began to grow on me. I grew to love to sing hymns—"This Little Light of Mine" and "All God's Children," among others. The spirituals helped me during my periods of hardship, although at times I wondered if the Lord could really hear me when I called to Him for help. I questioned whether He could be on my side if I was a mistreated child. And yet He guided me through these times in prayer, which became an important part of my life especially after this home, like the previous foster home, turned out to be no pleasure palace.

That summer, we took a family trip to Mrs. Jackson's home in the Carolinas for the weekend. The scenery was beautiful; the trees—some even looked blue—and the fields of corn were really something to see! It was July of 1967 and I remember the prejudiced attitudes the Jacksons faced in Delaware when stopping for fuel at gas stations along the way. At first, I didn't understand why we kept being turned away until I heard the gas attendant yell, "No niggers here!"

Finally, we came across a gas station that served us. Soon after, we arrived in Mrs. Jackson's home town. We drove up the narrow dirt road leading to the tattered, wooden plank-built house supported by four cement blocks. The first thing that came to mind was, who could live here? This was different from anything I could have imagined. While we unloaded the car, Mrs. Jackson and her sister greeted one another with cries of joy. Once settled in, I quietly excused myself. From the porch, where I went to sit, I watched the muddy creek which ran along the side of the house, separating the yard from the woods.

That night, the air was filled with the sounds of crickets and something which they called "buzzards," whose humming noise drove me crazy. I was eaten alive by huge mosquitoes which seemed to feed off me in particular. In the morning my eyes and mouth were swollen from the bites. I'd had enough! There was still another day to go in the sweltering heat. I decided I'd try to make the best of it.

Around midday, Mrs. Jackson's nieces and nephews offered to show me the town. I hesitated until one of the girls said, "C'mon girl, wanna go get some soda pop?" Having only the vaguest idea of what she was talking about, I went along in hopes of getting a 'pop'! The way to the store felt like a journey to Jordan. I grew tired. I turned to one of the girls and asked, "How far is it?"

"Oh, it's just down the road some."

Crossing the road, I spotted a snake. I yelled and hopped around, until one of the girls turned to me and said, "That thang ain't studin' you!"

I was definitely ready to leave now! We finally made it to the store, which turned out to be a small pump station with a soda machine that sat outside the door. This was where the kids hung out. Although I didn't get the ice pop that I expected, I began to enjoy listening to the way they spoke, and before I knew it I found myself speaking the same way.

The next morning around 8 A.M., we were on our way back to New York. But soon after we started out we had to stop on the side of the road because of mechanical problems. While waiting out in the heat, I wandered off into the bushes to find shade and stumbled on a beautiful orange and black turtle. I was afraid to pick it up. We played a cat and mouse game of sorts. Each time the turtle stuck its head out, I'd jump back. When it returned into its shell, I'd attempt to pick it up. Finally, I succeeded. At that moment, I gasped with excitement, the little feet crawled out of the shell. I flinched from the unexpected movement, not wanting to drop the turtle. I held it up and away from my body. I didn't want it to bite me and I didn't know what else it was capable of doing. Wanting to bring it back to New York with me, I needed something to put it in. I came across an empty peanut butter jar. I punched holes in the lid, but by the time we reached the Delaware border, Mrs. Jackson discovered that I had the turtle and ordered me to let it go. For the rest of the drive, I thought about the turtle, hoping it would find a cool place to lie and not get run over by a car. I thought it would survive.

After we got home later that night, things went back to what the Jacksons considered normal. The following day, Mrs. Jackson prepared for her son's visit home from the army. He and Linda were friends; they talked and exchanged information on what was going on here at home and what life was like in the service. We sat and listened to records. I liked snapping my fingers to "Jimmy Mack" by Martha and the Vandellas. In the evening, the Jacksons decided to go out. Their son left, too, so Linda babysat me. Linda, having plans of her own, took me along to a neighbor's house party. In a smoky basement lit only by two colored bulbs, one red and the other blue, I watched the teenagers kissing and hugging to the slow jams by the Moments and the Dells. I sat thinking to myself, this is boring. When I cried and complained to Linda, she pushed me aside. "Sit down," she said, "and shut up!"

Finally, we left. Before approaching the house, Linda warned me, "Don't say anything about where we were to Mrs. Jackson or I'll kick your ass, you hear?!"

"I won't," I said, scared to death.

On another occasion, one in which Linda left me wondering about her state of mind, Mr. and Mrs. Jackson were out shopping. Linda and I were left behind to clean the house. We began with our room. Linda started with her dresser; I straightened up the wardrobe closet which stood by my bed. Linda attempted to strike up a conversation, which was unusual. She normally acted as though I was more of a bother than a sister. But then she turned to me and asked, "Have you ever been with a boy?"

I looked up with a dumbfounded expression and said, "No." She continued with other questions about boys and sex. In my innocence, I responded with silence.

Shortly after, the Jacksons returned with the groceries. Mrs. Jackson was planning for the evening ahead with her friends. Later, when they arrived, I was in bed listening quietly to the laughter coming from the living room. Linda entered the room, restlessly turning the lights on and off, playing her radio just loud enough to keep me awake. As I was lying there on my side, with my back turned to her, trying to shade my eyes from the light, she whispered, "Pam, are you awake?" I didn't want to so much as blink for fear she would start pinching me. I hated this with a passion. I closed my eyes tightly. Finally, she turned the lights off. Then, before I knew it, Linda pounced on top of me. "This is what boys do: 'humping' and you better not tell either," she said, with her fist in my face. Linda felt threatened by my presence and used her greater physical strength to humiliate me. But to her, this also was my education, an introduction to her world of sex and boys.

After this upsetting introduction to sex, I would have bad dreams and roll into the wall next to my bed in my sleep. Mrs. Jackson stuck straight pins into masking tape and taped it to the wall. When I asked, "Why are you doing this?" she'd say, "This will stop you from damaging my walls." The tape was lined up along the wall, extending the length of my body, and during the night I would roll into it and awaken, startled.

One evening she caught me stripping the tape from the wall. She flew into a tantrum.

"I told you that I want this to stay! You're not fit to sleep in a bed!"

Each time the social worker came, Mrs. Jackson would remove the tape in fear that she might want to check my sleeping quarters.

In August I turned nine. And in September I re-entered the third grade. Since I was now a year older, and a little large for the third grade, I felt even less at ease than I had the previous spring. Then in December, as the weather turned freezing, a new social worker showed up. I never had the same caseworker twice; this seemed to be common practice. Mrs. Jackson called me into the living room where they had been discussing me.

"Hello, I'm Mrs. Rush," she said.

My eyes gleamed with relief when I saw that she was African-American—the first time I had ever been assigned to someone of my own race. Suddenly, I believed she was going to relieve me of this horror. As soon as Mrs. Jackson left the room, she began to question me on how things were going. At first I felt a bit reluctant to answer, due to my previous experiences with social workers. This visit, however, seemed different. After some time, I broke down and began telling her how Mrs. Jackson would make Linda and me go out into the yard at the side of the house and have switch fights to settle our disagreements. I said I believed Mrs. Jackson enjoyed this. Mrs. Rush then said I was lying. I pleaded with her to listen.

"Please get me out of here. I don't want to be here."

"What do you want?"

"I want to go home."

"Where is home?"

What more could I say but, "I don't know."

"You're too young to know what's good for you."

After telling her some more of what went on, it became clear that this social worker and this visit were not different. I felt shoved aside—what I had to say didn't matter. No one wanted to listen. I'd be passed off again as an imaginative child. No one should have to put up with this kind of treatment.

In February, 1968, in just under a year, my life in the Jackson home ended. The anonymous bureaucracy that controlled my life placed me in yet another foster home. This one was not far from Queens, in Long Island. Not knowing whether my complaints to the caseworker two months earlier had sparked the removal, I went along with it. At the time it seemed as if everyone blamed me for what happened. So I was surprised, years later, to find that the 'authorities' had on this occasion judged me more or less fairly. Perhaps behind her stern exterior Mrs. Rush had been responsive to my pleas after all.

> Pam did not do as well in this home as she had previously in placement. The home was not a beneficial one for her as the foster mother was not responsive enough to Pam's needs, leading to considerable sibling rivalry with the other foster children in the home.[2]

My new foster parents were Helen and Frank Harris. They lived in a two-story house with large front and backyards; in the front stood a huge weeping willow that swayed with the wind. Mr. Harris was a tall man in his late fifties with a very fair complexion and Mrs. Harris was in her late forties. Mr. Harris, originally from Georgia, enjoyed telling stories at dinner time of his childhood on a farm and I enjoyed listening. Mrs. Harris was very religious and had very little education. She believed religion played a strong part in childrearing. Through their Baptist Church, at the request of Mrs. Harris, I attended vacation Bible school every summer and sang in the Young People's Choir. My stay in the Harris home would last, with significant interruptions, five and half years.

On the face of it, this new home appeared upright and structured, even ideal. There were four other children in the home—two of them were foster care children like me. Mr. and Mrs. Harris insisted that I act as a sister to their granddaughter, Mae, and her brother, Ty. Mae and I were to share a bedroom. But something happened right off the bat that undermined my ability to trust the people responsible for my new home life. At the time of my transfer, Mrs. Rush, the social worker, came to the Harris's home. She and Mrs. Harris sat in the dining room talking. I overheard her telling my new foster mother my case history.

"Is there anything I should know about her?" Mrs. Harris asked.

"Well, yes, Pam is coming from a home in Queens, where she shared a room with a teenage girl. From what I can see, she's a problem child," Mrs. Rush stated.

"What about her parents? Any other relatives?"

"None have inquired about her. Of what I know, her mother drinks quite heavily and her father, after turning her over as a ward of the State, went on to remarry a

woman with five other children. The woman doesn't
want her."

This was the first I'd heard of any of this. Hearing that
my father was alive and had a family I could live with
made me regret being alive. I hated my father because he
cared for someone else before caring for me. I was only
one child! How could he leave me and allow me to go
through this with people who cared little about me?

Later, when Mae and I would get into spats, she
would throw this information, which her grandmother
had told her, back at me. Other times Mrs. Harris
would get into the act. It was as if the words "unwanted
child" were blazoned across the sky and branded into
my skin, giving others the right to treat me differently
than other people. "If the check from the agency doesn't
get here soon, I'll call the agency and tell them to get
you out of my house!" Mrs. Harris would shout at me.
When I needed new clothes or wanted the fashionable
clothing that the other kids were wearing, I would be
told that the agency only gives money for certain
things. "What you want they do not allow for, and I'm
not spending my money on you."

One of the other foster children at the Harris's was
Pete, who had lived with them for about three years. We
became close, realizing we were treated differently than
the Harris's blood relations. The rest of the children
enjoyed taunting Pete, calling him "Sambo" and making
fun of his dark complexion. I would counterattack by
making fun of their grandfather's very fair complexion,

calling him a "whitey." Mrs. Harris reacted quickly when she heard me on one occasion, stating, "Mr. Harris isn't a white man! He just has light skin, you heifer, you. I'll beat your black ass." Throwing her hands in the air, she commanded, "You get upstairs to your room."

I started up the stairs, then I decided to just stand there. No matter how hard she struck, I refused to cry, looking her in the face as if I could look right through her.

"What?! You won't cry? Oh, no! I'll beat you 'til you do! Harris," she yelled to her husband, "Look! She won't move!"

Growing tired, she eventually stopped. I went to my room as ordered and sat in the closet. When I felt depressed, that was where I'd go. Eventually I fell asleep. By the time I woke up, dinner was being served. I could hear Mrs. Harris yelling from the bottom of the stairs, "Pam!" I refused to answer, wanting to see if she'd miss me. My stomach growled as I heard the clanging of the dishes being cleared from the table.

"Where's Pam?" I heard Mr. Harris ask.

"I don't know and I don't care." Mrs. Harris replied. "I've called to her several times to set the table. She didn't come down, so the devil with her!"

The night drew nearer; it was eight o'clock. Still sitting at the table sipping Canadian Club, Mr. Harris said, "Did Pam come in yet?"

"I don't know!"

Suddenly, I heard footsteps coming towards the room. "Pam," said Mr. Harris in a heavy voice, "you come out of the closet. What the devil is wrong with you? Go downstairs and get something to eat. Come on, here!"

From that moment on, I knew he cared.

One day when the Harrises went out and left the oldest foster girl, Virginia, in charge, she called me into the kitchen to clean up the mess she and the other children had made. Mrs. Harris never gave me the opportunity to help prepare food. "The most you can do is set the table and wash the dishes," she'd say. When I refused to clean up the mess, Virginia slapped me.

My hatred grew stronger. My sentiment was, who was she anyway? She was placed here just as I was—unwanted.

Towards the end of my first year at the Harris's, Virginia left for college. She was replaced by Gina, another girl from the agency, who was seventeen. Gina was brazen. She smoked heavily and gave the impression of being a street person who enjoyed partying. She had a strong liking for older men and could be quite loud when expressing herself. When the Harrises were in bed, she would sneak downstairs and dip into the Canadian Club, which irritated Mrs. Harris, not so much for the expense, but for love of her own after-dinner drink. It got to the point where Mr. Harris began marking the bottle.

Other foster children came and went, like Lisa, a teenager who lived with us for a few weeks and then ran away to live with friends. After living in so many different environments, I reacted badly to the frequent changes in this one, even if it was my first lasting home environment. As I approached my tenth birthday I felt I no longer knew what to expect from one day to the next, or whom to trust.

The summer was drawing to a close and school was starting. The Harrises enrolled me in the Copiague school where I re-entered the third grade yet again. The previous school year I had been shifted from place to place and had not been able to complete the required school hours to move to fourth grade. At this new school, however, I didn't experience as many adjustment problems. The teachers were attentive and showed a willingness to work with me. School here was fun. I participated in music and sports activities and played the glockenspiel for the Christmas show.

Christmas 1968 was one I'll never forget. When I awakened, everyone was gathered in the living room. As I watched the others open their gifts, the distance I felt from them was magnified. Nonetheless, I was still bursting with the spirit of the season. I had asked for a record player or tape recorder. I opened my gifts and found slippers and a robe. As I looked around at the others, I grew enraged. I threw the box down. "I don't want nothing from you people!" I screamed and stormed up to my room.

Later on that evening, Mrs. Harris and the family sat laughing about the incident of the morning. I sat at the top of the stairs, listening.

"Well, Harris," she said, "the agency didn't send us any Christmas money for her. Maybe the social worker will have something. What are we supposed to do?"

Some weeks later, Mr. and Mrs. Harris came up to the school. I was called down from class for a meeting with the school's social worker who told me, "The Harrises are here today about you."

Mr. Harris asked, "Do you want to be adopted by us?"

"No," I said, shaking my head.

Nothing more was said. I guess I carried such bitterness within myself that I rejected anyone whose kindness and concern seemed in any way qualified or measured, rather than generous and absolute. Besides, Mrs. Harris's granddaughter Mae and I never really got along and I felt that sooner or later there would be conflict between us. She and her brother Ty made it clear that Pete and I were not a part of their family.

During the next few years at the Harrises I enjoyed occasional church socials, Papa's stories at dinner, singing along to records by myself in my room, or just dreaming. But what I remember most is the feeling of being slighted so often, and the sense of unfairness that I should be expected to accept so much less than what other children had. Every once in a while the Harrises would receive gifts from long time domestic employers of Mrs. Harris. When the secondhand clothes or whatever arrived, their grandchildren were able to go through the things first, and whatever they didn't want, Pete and I could have. I always refused. I didn't want leftovers; I'd rather do without. Mrs. Harris made it clear that the things were meant for Mae and Ty. Yet when it came time for the household chores, Pete and I did more than our share.

On many occasions, what I took to be the Harris's dislike for me devasted me. Once someone marked up the upholstery of the family car with a magic marker. Having no idea what had taken place, Mrs. Harris called me from my room and questioned me.

"Come down here right now! What do you know about this?"

"Nothing," I said.

"You did this, didn't you?"

"No."

"Oh, yeah! You're no damn good. You're just like your mother and she is no damn good and that's why you're here, you heifer!"

On many occasions, I would return from school to find all of my belongings strewn about my bed. She would actually take my dresser drawers and turn them over on my bed and as if that weren't enough, she'd take the clothing hung up in the closet, and dump it on the

floor. Each time I'd enter my room and find this awaiting me, my anger was reflected in my tears. I couldn't
understand why she would treat me this way.

But as I grew older, Mrs. Harris did begin to assign
me certain duties. She would take infants on a short
term basis—for a year or more—depending on how
long it took the agency to find permanent guardians.
The babies slept in the room upstairs next to my room.
I particularly enjoyed one baby boy. Every now and
then I would be allowed to stay home from school
to look after the child so the Harrises could run er-
rands. During the night, I'd be the one to get up and
care for him when he needed to be changed. Mr. Harris
nicknamed me "the second mother." None of this really
bothered me, because it felt good to care for another
in ways that I could never recall being cared for myself.

Mr. Harris and the boys would tinker around with
tools and leave objects lying around. "Papa," as we
called him, was a sportsman, and enjoyed hunting.
Sometimes, being absent-minded, he would leave gun
shells lying on his dresser in the bedroom, along with
various other objects. Well, one day, Mrs. Harris went
upstairs to get the baby from his nap and found nails in
his crib. She screamed; we came running.

"I'll kill you!" she said to me. "You're crazy! You
tried to kill the baby."

I stood there, puzzled as to what she was talking
about. "I don't know what you're saying."

"Someone put nails in here, and no one did this but you." There was no room to explain because she was rambling on. I was being blamed. I thought, Why not? I served no real value to them, only dollar signs.

> Pam adjusted well to this home and continued to function positively until 12/71 when her behavior changed abruptly, alternating between passivity and withdrawal to disruptive aggressivity. In the following months, Pam became increasingly negative and hostile toward the other children in the home, showing great jealousy of them and the attention they received. More and more, she felt left out and unwanted. She has requested removal from this home as she was so unhappy.[3]

This time the consequences for me were severe. The new social worker, a woman named Miss Austin who had replaced Mrs. Rush, instructed Mr. Harris to take me to the emergency room of Elmhurst General. On the way to the hospital I tried to tell Papa that I didn't have anything to do with what had happened.

"What are they going to do with me?" I asked him.

"I don't know," he said, "I guess they will examine you."

When we arrived, I froze. While we waited to see the doctor, a tall African-American man was escorted in by two policemen. He had been knifed! I began to shake uncontrollably. The man was wearing a pink pinstripe shirt and the blood was running from the gashes in the shirt where he had been stabbed. Papa could see the fear in my face. I begged Papa, "Please don't let them keep me here."

"We'll see what happens after you see the doctor. Your social worker wants you to be seen."

Tears were streaming down my face. The psychiatrist then called me in to ask me questions like "Who is the President?" At the time, Richard Nixon was and I answered that and other questions satisfactorily. Afterwards, he called Papa in alone. I sat quivering, waiting for word as they decided my fate. Finally, Papa came out and said, "Let's go home."

From then on, not wanting to spark any trouble, I tried to keep "out of sight, out of mind." I'd go to my girlfriend's house, around the corner. It was comfortable there. Her parents were pleasant when I would call on her to come out to play or talk. Talking to Kena, I found out that she knew how to sew and was making some summer clothing.

"Mae's got a sewing machine, but I can't use it to learn. Mae acts like no one can touch it," I told her.

Kena offered to teach me with the help of her older sister. Hours later, I had completed a pants suit. Overjoyed with a sense of accomplishment, I planned to wear it when we marched in the Memorial Day parade.

Three months later, according to records, Mae and I got into an argument over who had really marked up the interior of the car for which I had been blamed. A

fight broke out between us and, it was reported I tried
to kick her to death on the living room floor. That day,
as I remember it, she was getting the better of me and
the damn dog kept snapping at me. When the fight
spilled into the kitchen, I grabbed the first thing I could
get my hands on, which happened to be the carving
knife, and I went after her. I wanted Mae to leave me
alone. She was good about starting things and I was
tired of it and the whole damn mess. She had something
to do with the incident and I wasn't going to be blamed,
no matter who she was protecting. Papa broke up the
fight, but I was still seething. Waiting for her to leave
her room, I entered and cut up a few pieces of clothing
at random.

> She was seen psychiatrically in March, 1972, at
> ----- following an incident of threatening and
> chasing the foster mother's grandchildren with a
> carving knife.[4]

I went back to Elmhurst General, this time for thirty
days of observation. When I was taken to the psychiatric ward on the tenth floor, I grew silent. The rooms all
had locks and bars on the windows. The nurse took me
to the last room on the left side of the hallway where
I was to share a room with one other girl. The ward
had a cold, clammy feel to it. Painted in a dull green
with cement walls, the beds were hard with old iron
frames.

"This is where you'll sleep. Here's a toothbrush and paste. I'll call down for sheets," a nurse said.

Standing there for a moment looking around, I studied the thickness of the walls and the one window. I walked over, pressing my forehead against the gates which barred me from seeing anything other than the barbed wire fence surrounding the three top floors. Returning with the stiff sheets, the nurse said, "You can make your bed later, come with me for now!"

"Can't I sit in here?"

"I'm afraid not. The doors are kept locked during the day."

Walking towards the nursing station, I noticed the other patients returning from school.

"O.K., Pam. You come sit here at this table. I'm going to take your blood pressure and temperature before the next shift comes in."

"Do I have to get a needle?"

"Why?"

"I don't really want to."

"Well, not this time, but you'll have blood work done sometime next week."

While she checked my pressure, I glanced around the room at the others who each seemed like they were floating in a stupor. One flopped down in front of the television as though it would kill her if she stood any longer. The others gathered at the three tables like flies dropping from the ceiling in total exhaustion. Suddenly, a loud clang sounded. I jumped.

"Relax, it's only the dinner bell that lets us know the food truck is on its way to our floor. You're finished now! The rest of you line up for medicine," she said, calling each by name, one at a time.

One resident noticed me still sitting there, refusing to move from that spot. I was feeling as if I'd had something and then lost it, as though I'd lost my best friend. "What's your name?" she said.

"I don't know," I said, trying to avoid her, "Why?" I was saved by the arrival of the food truck.

"O.K.! Everyone to your place. You, too," the nurse said, tapping me. "I can't open the door until everyone is seated."

Dragging myself to a chair, I plopped down.

"What's for dinner?" someone screamed in my ear.

"It's fish," the nurse answered.

"I can't eat," I said, feeling as though I had hit rock bottom. I was unable even to lift the top off the food. Sobbing in pain and loneliness, feeling that I was being punished for something I didn't do, I buried my head in my chest.

That night I lay huddled in a self-embrace, rocking in motion, humming the tune "Kumbyah, My Lord." Soothing my soul, I fell off to sleep.

The next morning at 7 A.M., I was awakened by the jingling of the keys entering the locks and the voice of a nurse.

"Wake up! Time to hit the showers!"

Crawling out of bed, I slightly scraped my thigh on the springs.

"Ouch!" I said.

"You O.K.?" my roommate inquired.

"Yeah. Where are the showers?"

"Down the hall. You'd better get your things 'cause some of these people are nasty. They spit and pee in the shower."

Having only the things I came in with, I didn't have much to gather. When we reached the line, only three girls were ahead of us. I listened to them expressing their hopes of leaving soon and telling stories of their boyfriends, but what most surprised me was having to take a shower with others watching.

Then it was my turn. Stepping into the stall, I noticed the last person's hair had clogged the drain and flooded the floor.

"Where's my towel?" I shouted, as the nurse came running with a sheet.

"Dry off with this," she said, handing me one.

When I entered the dining area, breakfast was being served: runny eggs with greasy bacon.

"Never mind, I'm not hungry," I said.

The nurse said, "When breakfast is over, the doors will be unlocked and chores will be assigned. Pam, you'll clean the utility room."

I found that the utility room stored the washing machines and the refrigerator for snack time. I was more concerned with being able to wash my clothes. "Thank goodness," I thought.

Later, I sat in the corner of the room, attempting to isolate myself from the others, overhearing one resident whispering to another, "I hope they open the wards tonight."

"Yeah!" said the other. "I can't wait."

Following the routine that night, the wards were open for socializing and the girls were allowed to go over to the boys' side.

"Do I have to go?" I asked.

"No, I'll be sitting right here watching," the nurse assured me.

"Can I sit here?"

"Yes."

Looking down the hall, I could see the sights: Some could barely speak for the saliva drooling down the sides of their mouths as though they were chewing lard. One of the so-called couples sitting just outside the ward decided to sneak a kiss. I thought to myself, What goes on here? Neither the nurse nor the attendants see this?

Open wards lasted for an hour. Then it was snack time. The wards were locked, the utility room opened. I hadn't eaten for two days and hunger had set in.

"What's for snack?"

"Tuna or grilled cheese."

Enjoying fixing my own food, I ate tuna fish on buttered toast and grilled cheese sandwiches. Before long, I felt fat and sluggish, stuffing my worries away.

The next day, the doctor, whom I hadn't seen yet, prescribed Thorazine—50 milligrams dosage, twice a day. Within forty-eight hours, I became a zombie. Drugged, I could barely speak, my speech slurred. I became like the others.

One Saturday night while lying in my bed, I heard the nurses bringing in a thirteen-year-old girl from a party where she had been slipped some LSD. She was experiencing a bad trip. None of the residents saw her again until that Monday. She had been in seclusion to keep her from harming herself or others. When they let her out, the drug hadn't quite worn off, so she walked around the unit claiming to be picking up meat. She made her way to me saying, "Give me my 007 gun." I looked at her in amazement, not knowing how to respond. I stood with my mouth open. The nurse then came to sit her down but she pulled away. Not being able to control her, the nurse called for help and two other attendants came with a restraining jacket, better known as a straight jacket. After seeing this, I vowed never to take any drugs.

I attended what they called school here at Elmhurst on the twelfth floor from 9:00 A.M. to 2.30 P.M. Classes included arts and crafts, along with some remedial studies in math and English. Taking arts and crafts was relaxing, although half the time I couldn't keep my eyes open and my movements were sluggish. I don't remember what we read in English, except that it was in a green, cloth-covered book. In arts and crafts, the other children from the ward were molding ashtrays from clay. I made a scroll of sorts on which I painted a poem that read in part "Don't build bridges you can't cross."

My nights were long and lonely. No one visited me, as the other residents' parents did. I felt as though no one gave a damn about me; I was nothing more than a forgotten child of no use to anyone. The only time I felt a sense of being alive was when I'd hear the song "I'll Take You There" by the Staple Singers on the radio. The lyrics lent me spiritual strength.

The residents were allowed, on certain days, to make phone calls. So I decided I would call the Harrises—being that they were the only ones I could call—in hope of relieving the depression I experienced when seeing the other residents receive visitors. It was the first time I had spoken to anyone outside the walls of Elmhurst. Mrs. Harris answered. I asked to speak with Papa, hoping to talk to him, knowing his sense of understanding. Mrs. Harris refused to call Papa to the phone.

"No, you'll stay where you are. He's not coming to get you," she said and hung up.

I often thought about the stories Papa told during dinner and the sayings from his childhood, which brought laughter to me at my lowest moments. "Don't count your chickens before they hatch" and "Don't put the horse before the cart." These memories, for a time, were all I had to hold on to. Mrs. Harris's refusal left me feeling bitter for being forgotten and considered worthless. I became so withdrawn that when the social worker came to visit, I refused to see her. She ignored my request to be left alone. When she walked through the locked doors, I could barely look her in the face, bitter and believing she was responsible for keeping me here.

"How are you doing?"

"Why don't you leave?" I said.

"It's my job to come and check on you."

"When can I leave this place?"

"To go where? I have no place for you. Most of the foster homes don't want thirteen-year-olds."

I became silent, wondering why. The social worker's purpose for being there that day was for a conference with the on-staff psychiatrist. Shortly after their meeting, I was called in. When I entered the room my heart began to pound, and I shook with fear.

I faced a team of psychiatrists and psychologists who were seated at a long table, which gave me the feeling of being on trial. Once I was seated, the preliminary questions were asked, like what my name was, date of birth, etc. They were attempting to see just how off in the head I was. Before long, the questioning shifted to incidents that had occurred at the Harris's.

"Did you try to kill Mrs. Harris's granddaughter?"

I tried to respond quickly, with my lethargic tongue, fearful another question would be asked before I had time to explain.

"Did you cut up Mae's clothes?"

"What?" I responded. "No!" It took so much effort to get the word out, I hardly knew which question I was answering.

When the tension in the room slackened, I asked, "When can I be released?"

"We'll see," one of the doctors answered. He then went on to explain what their expectations were for release. "You are here for observation for thirty days. You are expected to take your medication, attend classes and see the doctor you'll be assigned to twice a week. If you don't cooperate with these rules, you will prolong your stay here. The staff social worker will report to your B.C.W. worker on your progress. If you need anything, let the nurses know."

They left abruptly and I was taken back to the ward.

My biggest fear after this meeting was that they would request electric shock treatment, as they had with some of the other residents, who told horror stories of pain and humiliation. They would return exhausted. When the effects wore off, they showed us the bald spots on their heads, where patches had been cut and paste applied to keep wires in place. I was spared this insult, perhaps because of my age. I was thirteen and a half.

At the end of the thirty-day evaluation, instead of being sent back to the Harrises, I was sent to Queens Children's Center, part of a psychiatric facility in Queens.

CHAPTER 2

THE BLUE DOORS

It was a warm spring day when I arrived at the Children's Center in the company of my social worker, Miss Austin. The date was June 7, 1972, and I was already looking forward to my fourteenth birthday two and a half months away. The center was a large facility located opposite another psychiatric institution; gates divided the two complexes. I stood for a moment before entering. It seemed peaceful from the outside.

When we entered the lobby, a few of the younger children were playing. I noticed the cheerfully painted walls, with each corridor painted a different color. My social worker and I waited for about fifteen minutes. Miss Austin, walking about the place, discovered a display of arts and crafts by the residents: "Come take a look at the things they've made. Maybe you can make something too while you're here." I walked over towards the display with no enthusiasm whatsoever. I was more concerned with finding out what the outcome of this visit would be, praying for rejection, hoping that

43

there were no beds available. But to keep Miss Austin quiet, I glanced at the table and mumbled something in response to her comments. As we returned to our seats, the staff caseworker came out to greet us. I already felt like a year had passed. The butterflies I began to feel in my stomach reminded me once again of that familiar feeling of being on unfamiliar ground.

Miss Austin and I were taken into the administrative wing for orientation where I sat nervously in one office while Miss Austin completed the necessary paperwork for my admittance in another. About half an hour later, an attendant was called to escort me to the assigned unit. As I parted from Miss Austin, I felt as though the world had swallowed me up. Feeling deserted as we went through the corridors of the main floor, I remember a stillness about the place. There was no one walking around to break the eerie silence. When we approached the elevators, I spotted a room off to my right, where some of the residents were in a class of some kind. When I began to look the place over, I discovered that the rooms were made of cement blocks so thick that the noise the children were making could not be heard unless you were extremely close to the door. As we waited for the elevator, I had the feeling that I'd never leave this place the same person.

By now we had reached the assigned floor and I was shaking like a leaf. "Where are you taking me?" I asked the attendant.

"You'll be in the blue unit," he said.

Sure enough, the outside of the unit and the doors were blue. The attending aides, along with the nurse, greeted me. The nurse asked me into the nurses' station, where she took my temperature and blood pressure. I was then taken to a room where I would sleep by myself, which put me somewhat at ease.

The unit had a small dining area for snack time. We ate our three meals a day in a large dining room just outside the unit. After sitting for awhile in my room, staring out the window, crying silently and wondering what I had done to deserve this, feeling that the Lord had let me down, hating the world, and, in particular, everyone who had entered my life and then exited it, I decided to look around. The rooms were kept locked whether you were inside or not, day or night. I had already experienced this humiliation at Rockland, but encountering it again here affected me badly. When I reached the nurses' station, it was time for lunch.

"Line up! Lunch time! Form two lines!" the aide yelled. I watched as the residents shuffled their feet, gathering their trays and utensils, waiting for the line to move. The aides hurried them along; the one dining hall served the entire floor and could hold only two units at a time.

The blue unit consisted of about ten girls, where some of the others could have as many as twelve to fifteen girls. All were here for some reason: some for behavioral problems or for violent crimes against family members, others were the victims of violent crimes.

After lunch, we returned to the unit where it was time for medication. I had hoped that the medication that I had been taking at Elmhurst would stop, finally, here at Queens Children's. So when the others began to form a line, I went and sat down. The nurse came over to inform me that my prescription would be sent up before the night was over.

When the night shift arrived, I was called for evening medication. I tried to stall; I asked the night nurse what kind of medication I was taking and why it wasn't in pill form. She responded, "Just take it and I'll give you juice after." Thorazine at a dosage of 50–100 mgs. But on this night, I was given a double dosage to make up for the missed afternoon dosage and I could taste the difference. Since it was in liquid form, the medicine had a stinging taste and a numbing effect on the tongue. I detested having to take medicine of any kind and especially Thorazine, because I knew I didn't need it. What I couldn't understand was why some of the residents would willingly stand on line to be knocked out. Then I saw what happened when you gave a nurse "a hard way to go" about taking medication. The attendants would be called and regardless of where you were on the unit at the time, they would pull down your skirt or pants and administer the medication by injection.

Sometimes the attendants would take us outside to the playground located on the grounds. In the heat of the day, the medicine caused dizziness and shortness of breath. I would try to find a shaded area to sit in to avoid passing out. Days when the sun was strong, I couldn't open my eyes, let alone try to participate in activities. It's a frightening experience to struggle against a chemical reaction you have no control over, to find yourself losing the battle day after day.

Some of the residents would carry their radios with them. The song that stuck to me during this time was "Body and Soul" by Soul Generation. When sitting alone, I'd try to sing the song to keep from crying and, just for a moment, hearing it would take me away from all that was around me.

Thirty days after I entered the Children's Center, I noticed my vision had become blurred. I was in the day room watching "Soul Train" when the picture started getting smaller, then disappeared. I screamed to the attending nurse on duty.

"I can't see! Somebody help!"

"Go back and sit down," she said.

In order to do so, I had to slide down the wall until I hit the floor. I became dizzy and passed out. Sometime later the nurse woke me for lunch. I was still lying on the bare floor. She could see that I was over-medicated, but she insisted that I get in line with the other residents and enter the dining room. I ate what I could see. When lunch was over, the last things I recall seeing were the blue elevator doors—located just outside the dining room—closing. I screamed at the top of my lungs for help. No one did anything. The nurse ignored my plea and escorted me back to the unit. I couldn't see anything, not even shadows.

Not only had I lost my sight, but my menstruation as well. This side effect would last for three months, well beyond the roughly two-month period during which I was actually taking the drug.

Finally, in mid-August, still unable to see clearly, I was released. I returned to the Harris's because the social worker was unable to find another home for me. After the trauma of being at the Children's Center, anywhere else was fine with me for the time being. Once I settled in, an appointment was arranged for me to see the family physician to be checked. The doctor who examined me confirmed that the medication had been prescribed in too strong a dosage for a child my age and weight and ordered me to discontinue its use. When the social worker was notified of the doctor's diagnosis, she then decided that other forms of medication with milder effects could be administered.

My medication was changed to Stellazine pills. In a matter of days, my sight returned. No one knew that most of the time I threw the pill into the toilet when Mrs. Harris, after handing me the medicine, turned away. She, like so many others, believed it did some good, when all it did was leave me sluggish and unable to participate in school. The school eventually complained about my sleeping in class. If it were warm in the classroom I'd find myself nodding off without wanting to. The more I'd try to fight it, the more I'd be defeated. The teachers would just allow me to sleep. There wasn't much they could do about it. The only time I would awaken was if a classmate dropped a book or the school bell sounded. Since my dosage of Thorazine had been so strong, enough remained in my system to affect me long after I stopped the treatment, and the Stellazine, supposedly a lighter form of Thorazine, seemed only to add to the heaviness. When taken in pill form over an extended period, it can take anywhere from six months to a year after discontinuance for these drugs to leave your system.

> Pam has experienced much rejection in her lifetime with lack of stability with significant persons. While she was first removed from home at age four, one can speculate about the type of care she received prior to that with parents who had numerous personal difficulties as well as marital conflicts. Her interrupted foster home placements, save for the last one, were more a result of difficulties in the families than Pam's failure to adjust to her situations. She is a sensitive individual who is very mistrustful of others and of any behavior which can be interpreted as rejection. It appears as if she has behaved many times to bring such rejection on herself.[5]

Although I returned to the Harrises as I'd requested, I still felt a great deal of resentment and trusted no one.

The social worker arranged therapy sessions upon my discharge from the Children's Center, but I refused to talk with the therapist for fear that what I had to say would get back to Mrs. Harris. Week after week, we just sat there with him asking me questions and trying all sorts of things to help me open up. Finally, one day I opened up, feeling that maybe he could be trusted to understand what I had been through and to help me with the Harrises. I told him how the Harrises would have me and Pete, the other foster child, doing chores that their grandchildren didn't do, and how we were being treated as secondhand housemaids. As I had anticipated, the therapist called Mrs. Harris and told her of my conversation with him. When Mr. Harris and I reached home that night, she greeted me at the door.

"Listen," she said, shaking her finger in my face, "whatever goes on in this house is to stay here. It's none of their damn business."

So why send me to a therapist, if I'm not to express my feelings in confidentiality? The whole idea is to help one get a better understanding of one's emotions, isn't it?, I thought to myself as I walked to my room. I was trying to avoid blowing up at Mrs. Harris, and hating myself for being here or, for that matter, for being alive. She made me feel like I had taken something from her by going to the therapist. But it was Papa, not her, who was driving me. I believe that Mrs. Harris didn't want Papa showing an interest in me and sharing family matters with me during the ride—matters from which

Pete and I would normally be excluded. To her, the "motherless children," as she so often referred to us, only caused problems, while her grandchildren brought joy. Her willingness to accommodate *them* just shined.

During the next therapy visit, I refused to say a word. The doctor tried his damnedest to get me to open up; then I reminded him that he had phoned Mrs. Harris after he had said I should not be afraid because nothing would get back. I refrained from telling him what the result of his phoning the house had been. Later that evening, everything came together when I heard Mrs. Harris asking her husband, "Are they paying for the gas to take her back and forth?"

"Well, the agency will reimburse us for the mileage, something like 12¢ a mile."

"We can't afford this for a forty-five-minute visit. It takes that long just to get her to the therapy sessions."

He didn't say a word in response. Papa was a kind and caring person, even when being so placed a strain on his pocket. He was the type of person who would do for another if he thought it would benefit them in some way.

Having returned to the old routine, I entered the Copiague school's eighth grade class. I was ashamed to tell anyone who would ask where I had been, let alone what I had been through. Some of my schoolmates had drawn their own conclusions from circulating rumors that I was crazy or even homicidal, having had some help with their story from Mae and her friends.

Life in school was a battleground. Fighting became a means of survival. Classmates would tease me about my weight—anything to get a fight started. I survived that fall and winter, but one day in the spring, out of the blue during gym, one of the girls started flapping her gums about me and another girl's pimply faced boyfriend, whom I didn't like and who didn't like me. At the start of the next class, all hell broke loose. Nora, the girlfriend, threatened, "I'm gonna kick your ass!"

"What are you talking about?" I said.

She slapped me.

"You lowlife bitch," I said. I picked up my chair and threw it at her, missing, but not by much.

The teacher, Mr. G., came towards us with a shocked expression on his face. "I never heard girls use such language. Pam, you go to the office."

The tension filled the hallways for the rest of that day. My heart pounded at the sound of the seventh-period bell. I feared the sounding of the last bell of the day, still another forty-five minutes away, wondering what was going to happen then. As I walked through the corridors, I heard classmates whispering among themselves, "You gonna see the fight?"

"Yeah," one answered. "Nora's going to get her."

When the last bell sounded, I started the mile walk home. I had no one to walk with because my friend Shirley hadn't come to school this day and Mae attended the high school but couldn't care less. Nora and her friends from the senior high school across the street planned a full-scale jump, all of them meeting underneath the highway crossing. By the time I got there, Nora had about seven girls with her.

"Hey, Pam," one called.

"Yes?" I said, trying to move quickly.

"Now we'll see who's the bitch," they yelled. They crowded around and pulled me down to the ground by my hair. I was unable to defend myself alone against so many. Someone kicked me in the eye. I became frantic; I couldn't see. Then all of a sudden they were gone. I picked myself off the ground and headed home.

"What happened?" Mrs. Harris asked, when I got there, as if she didn't know! Mae had reached home before I did and told her everything. She looked at my eye, gave me some ice and that was it.

Later in the evening, I ran into Shirley on the way to the store.

"Pam, I heard what happened today. Don't worry," she told me.

I didn't know what she had in mind. The next day I went to school with a steak knife for protection, just in case they intended to try again. Once word reached Nora that I was carrying a weapon, she made sure the dean found out. I was called down to the office.

"Do you have a knife on you?" he demanded.

"Yes, but I'm not going to use it."

"Well, hand it over or I'll have to call in the authorities."

"O.K."

"You are suspended for the remainder of the school year for having it," he informed me.

I couldn't live this down. There was only one month remaining before summer vacation. I couldn't believe I had been caught. Where was the dean yesterday when I was getting my brains kicked out?

The next day Shirley stopped by the house on her way to school. Mrs. Harris didn't care for the likes of Shirley. She felt Shirley was trash. Mrs. Harris called me to the door with that look of righteous scorn on her face. Shirley spoke in a low voice, "Can you be up at the school at three o'clock? We'll meet at the overpass."

A little before three, as I reached the overpass, I recognized Shirley's brother Rolan standing under the street light. There was a crowd of people with him. Shirley had come to my defense! I had never seen half of these people before. Shirley had drawn together her cousins and friends from another Long Island township. They were carrying chains, sticks and pipes.

A few minutes after the last bell sounded, right on schedule, Nora and some of her friends appeared. The crowd surrounded them and started over the bridge.

"It's your chance to get her back!" a voice shouted at me. I froze. I couldn't do it. I didn't want to hurt her. At the blink of an eye, fights broke out to the right and left of me. Someone said the cops were coming. I definitely didn't want to get caught by the cops after I had already been dismissed from school. I ran home. No one asked

any questions when I got there and I didn't say anything either.

Two weeks passed and then something curious
happened. I was sitting in the dining room being tu-
tored in order to graduate with my class, when my
math teacher, Mr. Saso, called. He seemed to see something in me that the other teachers didn't. Perhaps it
was because he had a different outlook in general.
In class, he always seemed more relaxed than the
others, cracking jokes regardless of how corny they
sounded, and not seeming to mind whether we laughed
or booed him down. But today he called asking
Mrs. Harris's permission for me to participate in the
class trip.

"O.K." she said. "Here's Pam."

"Do you want to go?" he asked me.

"Yes."

"Good, then this is what you'll do. Be at the school
next Friday by 8:30 A.M."

"But I'm not allowed anywhere near the school."

"Don't worry, O.K.? I'll handle it."

I showed up the day of the trip. Mr. Pettie, my
homeroom teacher, and the whole class were lined up
outside awaiting my arrival.

"O.K.," Mr. Pettie yelled, "let's get on the bus."

"This feels pretty sneaky," I whispered to Shirley.

"Duck down in the seat," Shirley said. "Hurry, the
dean is coming to wish us well."

I couldn't help snickering. Everyone was in on the act. The dean gave the longest speech in history and then decided to count heads.

"O.K., have a good time," he concluded.

As we pulled away, I popped up and the whole bus burst out laughing. I was as happy as a lark.

Fortunately the dean relented and, with one week remaining before summer break, I was allowed to return and completed the year with passing grades. A few days later I participated in the Junior High school commencement exercises. On graduation day I recall feeling shy about walking up to receive my certificate. I tripped on my dress on the way down and, feeling quite embarrassed, ran back to my seat. I heard about it all evening. "You acted like a damn fool up there today!" Mrs. Harris commented.

But at the Harris's nothing seemed to change. The tormenting statements made by Mrs. Harris and Mae, about my family members as though they knew them personally, wore on me. My own knowledge of my relatives was so scant that I could hardly defend myself. Protecting the only lasting memories I had, good and bad, kept me continually on the defensive. Mae and Mrs. Harris were always letting me know how much was theirs and how little was mine. They made sure I was the outcast. And it was the same for Pete, who they picked on for his complexion and his stammer. We were a sideshow to them, a form of entertainment. The favoritism was blatant. It was O.K. for Mae and Ty to attend school functions or to represent the family at church socials, but we weren't good enough. Mrs. Harris also had an irritating way of singling me out. She would often say, "You're not going to embarrass me." Even when it came to such little things as making out the grocery list: "Where's Mae? ,I want her to make up the list." She would totally dismiss my presence as if I didn't exist.

With summer, Mrs. Harris's games grew even worse. She often harassed us about the finances, complaining about the check for our upkeep being late. One day I called my social worker and said, "Please take me out of here." It wasn't the first time she had received a call requesting removal from the Harrises. But this time she seemed responsive.

"I'll be out to see you soon," she said.

About a week or so later, she came to the house. After speaking to both Pete and me separately, she said, "I'm going to work on it."

Two weeks later, she called Mrs. Harris to say she was removing us in two days. This gave Mrs. Harris little time to get back at me for the complaints I had made but she did her worst.

Pete, being thirteen at the time, went to a facility in upstate New York from which he later went on to attend Boston University, graduating with a bachelor's degree in photography. Pete and I lost track of one another after a while.

Pamela's request for removal from this home has
been known for over a year. She's been very un-
happy there, feeling left out as the foster parents
obviously favor their natural grandchildren over
Pam and another foster child as well as being
angry for the unkind things they had said to her
about herself and her family background. Contact
with B.C.W. indicates that some of Pam's resent-
ments are justified as the foster parents have not
been consistently sensitive or responsive to her
needs.[6]

During this period in my life, the bitterness and dis-
content I had felt for so long seemed to harden inside
me. My fears of becoming blind lingered. Never had I
experienced love in the true sense, never was I held or
cuddled as most children are. So I had to depend on
myself for the peace that others draw from their families
and I continued to hope that someone with a caring
heart would be able to take me into their home.

CHAPTER 3

MEANS OF SURVIVAL

Once Miss Austin had settled Pete in his new home, the boys' residence in Middletown, New York, she came for me. On the first Saturday in August, 1973, which happened to be a very warm day, we drove through bumper-to-bumper traffic on the Belt Parkway and then crossed the East River from Brooklyn to Manhattan. Our destination was a temporary shelter for wayward girls on the East Side called Euphrasian Residence. At the age of fourteen-going-on-fifteen, this would be my fourth institutional shelter placement. The first thing I noticed when we arrived was how posh the brownstone building looked, like a private residence or a doctor's office. We entered and were asked to wait in the visiting room. There, in an early colonial setting with high ceilings and marble halfway up the walls, my palms were sweating from anticipation and the heat. I momentarily escaped the uneasy feeling by asking questions.

"This is nice. I like this! How long will I be here?"

"You'll be here for thirty days," replied Miss Austin.

"Oh! And then where will I be?"

"I'm not sure. Well, it's time to go in."

After a brief introduction, Miss Austin parted, wishing me well. My new home was run by Catholic nuns and it seemed peaceful, even though there were about twenty girls living on each of the two floors. On the second floor, where I was assigned, were younger girls ranging from thirteen to sixteen years of age. On the third floor, the older group was assigned.

The sister assigned to my floor, tall but narrow in frame, gave me a tour explaining the point-scale system of rules.

"The rooms are broken down into categories by the style of furnishings. The first is colonial, painted in a lively pink; second is contemporary, painted in lime green; third is traditional in lavender, and last, in palest white, Euphrasian arms. The girls who've been here the longest and have earned the right to their own rooms, stay here in this wing."

"Oh! I like the colonial or traditional."

"Yes, but there's no room for you, so you're assigned to contemporary."

Sister, bending my ear to say a few more things, added, "Some of the girls here steal from one another, so keep an eye open . . . Oh, my goodness!"

Just as she completed the sentence, a fight broke out in the day area over a blouse one girl claimed had been taken from her room by another girl who had been ironing it.

Later I asked, "Why do they steal?"

"Well, some of them feel that it's the only way they can get what they want. It's easier than asking."

Oh no, I said to myself, thinking that I'd have to stand guard over what little I had.

"Some of the girls are placed here through the courts, others are here voluntarily like yourself," Sister said. Ending our conversation, she went on, "It's time for dinner. O.K., girls?"

"Do we set the tables?" I asked.

"Not down here—upstairs in the dining area."

"Where's that?"

"Seventh floor."

"Do we take the elevator?"

"No, the stairs."

"Oh goodness, by the time I get there, I won't want to eat."

When I reached the dining room, I thought I'd collapse. But the foods smelled good!

"What's for dinner?" I asked.

"Shrimp creole with rice."

"Sounds good!"

"Yes, but you'll have to help clean up."

"Never mind, then."

"You'll still have to help whether you eat or not and tomorrow's Sunday. You'll be given a chore for the week." Wouldn't you know it? I was given mopping those stairs from the seventh floor down!

On Sunday, after chores were completed, most of the girls left.

"Where's everyone going? Can I go?" I asked.

"No. When you've earned a pass, you'll be allowed to go with them on outings with the recreational counselors. In the meantime, the canteen is open," said a girl named Anna.

"Where's that?"

"Right here."

"Where?"

"That closet. You can buy candy, cigs, soda and yarn."

"I don't have any money."

"When your social worker from the agency comes, let her know."

"I don't know when that'll be! What kind of trips do we go on?"

"Well, we go roller skating and sometimes up to the farm."

"Can you go out?" I asked Anna.

"Yeah, but I wanted to stay here and crochet a blanket for my baby. See?" she replied, patting her stomach as she began crocheting.

"Wow! You do that so fast! How did you learn that?"

"Sister taught me."

"Yeah? Can you teach me?"

"O.K. Got yarn and a needle?"

"No."

"Here, I have an extra one and here's some yarn. It can get boring, but it keeps your mind off things. I don't miss my baby so much when I'm doing this."

"You have another baby?"

"Yeah, he's so cute. What about you?"

"Oh, no."

"Most of the girls here do. So what are you doing here?"

"Well, I was living with foster parents."

"Oh, I know. You don't have to say anymore. That's where my son is. At night I get to thinking about him and just cry."

Before I knew it, the others were returning.

"Oh, it was so quiet while you were out," Anna said to them.

During that first week away from the Harrises, I'd call from time to time because having someone to call on—wanting to believe I did—helped me feel less alone.

"Hello," Mrs. Harris answered, "who is this?"

"Pam."

"Oh, how are you doing?"

"Fine."

"What do you want?"

"Can I speak to Papa?"

"Look, let me tell you something. It was only because of you that Pete had to be moved."

"Well, Pete didn't have to go either. Nobody forced him. Have you spoken with him?"

"Yeah, he's O.K. He wants Papa to get him a bike. Papa says he's gonna get him one. By the way, Pam, Lady was hit by a car."

"What happened?"

"Oh, he got loose."

"Is he O.K.? Can I speak with Papa?"

"No!"

I knew she was telling me things about Pete and Lady, their dog, that would make me feel envy or guilt, rubbing salt in an open wound.

"You don't really care. All you're concerned about is the money," I complained.

"Well, we have bills to pay and Papa's retiring soon."

I hung up, plopped down on the couch and just sat there. Calling me from the kitchen area, Sister said, "Pam, you O.K.?"

"Yeah."

"Would you like to help me?"

Dragging my feet across the floor towards her with a "yes-and-no" attitude, I said, "Whatcha doin'?"

"I'm preparing yeast for bread."

"Bread? You make the bread?"

"Sometimes, as a treat. It's simple. Want to help?"

"Yes! Are you gonna bake it tonight?"

"No, tomorrow, after chores are done, for those of you who may want to stay behind. The Recreational department is taking the girls roller skating Saturday, but some of the girls will not be allowed to go."

Thinking back on their physical conditions, I understood. "Well, I want to bake bread!"

Saturday morning wake up call was at 7 A.M.

"O.K., girls, hit the showers!"

Everyone gathered their things to stand on line, waiting for a stall and for Sister to turn on the main valve. I had never felt comfortable showering in the open. The shower stalls were of grey and black marble with dividers six inches thick. Once I finished washing and had dried off, I wrapped myself in my towel and headed back to my room to get dressed. Sister, who normally stood guard, left for a split second—enough time for Claireese to smack my towel down. I slapped her into the shower divider just as Sister came back and caught me.

"There will be no fighting here or you'll not be allowed to stay here! Do you understand?"

"Yes, but she. . . ."

"Never mind."

Claireese stood in wonderment, recovering from the shock of my retaliation. My roommate came over and said, "You know, Claireese is a lesbian."

"Oh?" I said. "What's that?"

"She likes girls."

"Well, if she puts her hands on me again, she'll be a dead one."

"I don't think she'll try it anymore 'cause you stood up to her but you have to watch some of the girls.

Once breakfast was over, I sat in the day room listening to the others and crocheting. My first week there had passed. I no longer felt like the newcomer.

"Pam," Sister called, "are you ready to make the bread?"

"O.K."

"What happened this morning?" she asked after we measured out the flour, sugar and yeast in the kitchen area.

"Well, Claireese smacked my towel off."

"Claireese has been here the longest. They're unable to place her because of her ways, so she feels that nothing she does will make a difference. Try and stay away from her."

"When will I be able to go out?"

"Next week. I'm going to take the girls upstate to the convent and the farm for swimming. You'll come along then."

I can't swim, I thought to myself.

The days of the second week passed without incident. I learned which girls to keep my distance from by the way they carried themselves. Their street talk was a sure indication that they were tougher than me. Observing them made me realize that I was no longer in the protective shell of a middle-class neighborhood. I would now be educated for survival inner-city style, which meant knowing who could be intimidated and when to be invisible. In some ways, it wasn't any more than being able to send a strong message from the corner of your eye, enough to show the person intimidating you that you're not the person they'd want to mess with. Or you simply play crazy, getting in the person's face, bad breath and all. In large facilities it's a do or die situation; in smaller ones like Euphrasian it isn't as bad.

Meanwhile, on Friday the caseworker assigned to me here finally arrived.

"Hello, Pam, come in. Have a seat. Now, what did you want to see me about?"

"Getting out of here. Can you find a foster home for me with no other children?"

"Well, it will be hard because of your age. Most people don't want teenagers, but I'll try."

"Thank you. Can it be done before my birthday next week?"

"We'll see. O.K.? How do you like it here? You've been here now for two weeks. Having any problems with the others?"

"Why?"

"Well, from the reports, you don't seem to interact much with the others."

"Well, keeping to myself I stay out of trouble."

"Sister says you'll be able to go out tomorrow, O.K.?"

The next morning, we all piled into the station wagon. On the way to the farm some sang songs. I gazed out the window in wonderment: The further we got from the city, the better the scenery. Some trees were still in full bloom in mid-August. I remember the mimosa in particular. Large homes sat up in the hills on huge plots of land. The air was fresh and the skies were clear. We had left far behind us the stench and the smog of the hazy, hot city when I exclaimed, "Where are we now?"

"We're entering the Catskills."

"This is beautiful! Wow! I wish I lived up here."

Finally arriving at the farm, after sitting for God knows how long, I was glad to get out and stretch my legs. There were trees all around and horses grazing on the grass. We all dove in different directions.

Following Sister into the stables, I found one girl petting a horse.

"Come, you can pet the horse," the girl said.

The horse snapped at me, and I backed away.

"Oh, come on! He don't bite."

"Yeah! He's got teeth, right? Then he bites."

"He's friendly."

I eased over, attempting to touch him while his head was down. He began nibbling at my pants.

"That's it! I'll just stay out of his way! He's beginning to buck."

I quickly shuffled out of the gate.

"Where are you going?"

"This is close enough for me, outside this fence."

Growing tired and bored sitting by a creek that was nearby, I cast pebbles waiting for the others coming out of the pool.

We returned to the city in the evening.

Sister asked, "So, how did you enjoy the trip?"

"All right. I don't swim but I enjoyed the ride."

On Sunday, there were visiting hours for the residents. Feeling left out and lonely, I slipped into a corner unnoticed, knowing better, but still half expecting a surprise visit from no one in particular. Practicing my new-found skill, crocheting, as fast as I could, I tried to ignore the others bubbling over with excitement about seeing family and friends. I was waiting for Monday to request a meeting with the worker to see if she had come up with any homes. There were a few days left before my birthday and I was growing restless.

I met with Miss Austin once again.

"Well, there's nothing much to tell you—I have not found a place for you. I think it's best that you be placed in a facility with girls your own age."

"No! That's not what I want," I replied, fearing having to go back to the Children's Center or some place like it. "Please, can you get me out of here?"

"I'll continue to try. See you next week."

My birthday came and went without even a card and certainly no visitors. It turned out to be very depressing. Most girls look forward to their fifteenth birthdays. I had looked forward to mine too, but when it came there was nothing to celebrate.

Another week passed and then my life changed again. Miss Austin found a foster home for me in Queens.

"It's understood that you'll be there on a trial basis."

"Are there any other children?"

"No, just the woman and her husband. You'll be leaving here on Friday. The house is large and you'll have a room all to yourself."

Sounds perfect, I thought to myself. Thrilled about leaving, I crocheted an oval rug to give to my new foster parents.

Mrs. Richardson seemed pleasant when we first met. She was a middle-aged woman, on the stout side. She greeted us in a pleasant manner. But that wasn't unusual, because they all seem O.K. until you get to know them. When we entered the two-story brick house, I noticed the deep mahogany paneling in the living room with the window shades pulled to keep the sun's rays out, allowing the house to be kept cool. It all seemed ideal. There were no other siblings living in the home to bother with.

Mrs. Richardson offered Miss Austin and me a glass of iced tea. I refused, attempting to be polite. Instead, I presented to Mrs. Richardson the rug I had made. She accepted it with a "Thank you." And Miss Austin and she began their conversation on my case history, a story I had heard time and time again. The next item on the agenda was the school I would be attending. Mrs. Richardson had not dealt with the school system in a long while so that she had no idea which school zone she lived in. But I had my mind set on Andrew Jackson which was known among the girls to have some of the best-looking boys. In the living room sat Mrs. Richardson's beautiful piano. She spoke willingly of having a piano teacher come in to instruct me how to play it.

I entered the ninth grade at Martin Van Buren High School. At the time, schools in Queens were having racial problems, so I attended class on a split session, from 12:00 to 6:00 P.M. The grade counselor looked over my records with my foster mother while registering me.

"We're going to place you in eleventh grade biology and tenth grade math," the counselor said.

"Yes, but I'm only a ninth grader."

"Your records indicate advanced studies."

"Oh," I said, thinking, Wow! to myself.

But at the first class, I felt my stomach turning over. These kids were going to chew me up and spit me out. They were all older than me. I'll just keep quiet, I thought, until I answered a question from the text and got it right. The shock of it left me speechless.

When the class concluded, one classmate asked me, "How old are you?"

"Fifteen."

"So what are you doing in here?"

"They assigned me here."

"Well, you're all right."

Dreading the rumors I'd heard of the riots that would take place once school let out and knowing no one, I was terrified. Stories circulated of girls fighting with ice picks and chains, and placing razor blades in their afros to keep their opponents from pulling their hair. I figured, if I can make it each day to the 165th Street terminal to catch the bus home without any confrontations, I'm doing good.

After I'd lived with the Richardsons for two weeks, Mrs. Richardson and I set out early one Saturday morning for the beauty parlor she owned. Before the shop opened for business, I was to clean up and she was going to wash, press and curl my hair. But before leaving the house, I discovered her sipping her cherished daily pick-me-up—Scotch on the rocks. This worried me, to say the least, as I was to be her first customer of the day.

"Come on, girl, let's go. I'm going to do your head first before any of my appointments arrive," she said.

Scared to death that she might burn me while pressing my hair with the hot comb, I dragged along. Sure enough, with all my twitching and jumping from the heat of the hot comb, she got me.

"Oh! Did I burn you?"

"Yes!" I wondered how she could do anyone's hair when she started drinking so early in the morning. I couldn't say anything to her—she was twice my size and I felt she might slap me for speaking out.

That weekend, a friend from Long Island wanted me to go to the movies. I asked Mrs. Richardson, "Can I go to the movies?"

"Where?"

"Out in Long Island with one of my friends."

"O.K."

"What time should I return?"

"Eleven o'clock."

"O.K., but the show starts at eight and I'm not sure what time the next train back will be leaving."

"Well, use your better judgment."

But things went badly. When I reached the train station, I halted in my tracks. The trains were delayed. I had been given the warning to use my "better judgment." What would I do now?

While I was waiting on the platform, it began to pour. I figured I'd better turn around and head home. At about 11:30, Mrs. Richardson greeted me at the door.

"I told you, you hussy, to be back in time!"

"Yes, but I didn't go. The trains were delayed and the buses are runnin' slow. What did you want me to do?"

"Well, you won't go out again! By the way, your worker called. She'll be here on Monday."

When Miss Austin arrived on Monday, I was in my room upstairs. She had come bearing bad news.

"Your mother died, two weeks ago or so."

After she lowered the boom, I flopped down on the bed with a blank expression and asked, "When?"

"August 20th," she answered. "How do you feel?"

I hunched my shoulders, feeling no emotion, having no memory of her and not knowing whether I resembled her in any way. I was frightened somehow, because I didn't know her and now I would never know her. I was distraught, thinking that I should have been told sooner, in time to have been able to attend the funeral. This omission seemed to be the most inhuman thing any displaced child could have to endure. In the background I could hear the radio on my nightstand playing Marvin Gaye's "What's Going On?" What did it matter?

Not knowing what else to do or say, I changed the subject to Mrs. Richardson's drinking problem. To my surprise, Miss Austin had already picked up on it and was in the process of arranging for a transfer.

Several days later, she returned to help me pack my bags and we left.

> She was later placed at another foster home which did not work out because the foster mother proved to be an alcoholic. Pam was then placed at St. Michael's.[7]

Normally, the routine of being shifted from place to place didn't phase me enough to make me ask where I was going. But this time I did, and Miss Austin answered, "You're going to a place for adolescents."

"Where?" I continued.

"I'm not quite sure just yet, but first we'll have to stop at the agency. I have to make a few phone calls."

She really didn't have a place for me. We returned to the Bureau of Child Welfare in Queens. Being familiar with the bureau, I knew what to expect. I walked through the dull painted corridors with the frail woman known to me as my social worker, who was attempting to show compassion. We took the stairs to the fourth floor because the elevators weren't working. The air conditioner was out as well, and the doors on each landing stood open against the heat. As we climbed the stairs, I listened to other children who stood in the corners crying, waiting; and I wondered where they'd sleep tonight. This was the control center for all displaced children—some here through court order, some runaways or temporarily removed from their natural homes. The social workers and supervisors decided your fate.

I was hungry and it was lunchtime. Miss Austin's timing could not have been better when she turned and asked, "Are you hungry?"

"Yes."

While she called out for some hamburgers, I sat there wondering, would she forget to call for placement and let me go home with her? No chance of that, though. I watched her run from one department to another trying to obtain an agency reference book. About twenty minutes or so after she began, she returned to the desk with a huge, 600-page tome. As she thumbed through it, I couldn't imagine what it could have to do with me. Then she began placing calls, trying to beat the clock. It was now about 3 P.M. Nothing had turned up yet. She waited for other agencies to return her calls. About 30 minutes later, a call came in from a facility that had a bed and was willing to take me in on an emergency basis. But now we had to wait for approval and signature from a supervisor who hadn't yet returned from lunch. Miss Austin continued to gather the necessary paperwork. At around 4 P.M., our journey began.

CHAPTER 4

SAINT MICHAEL'S

September 21, 1973. We were on our way, by route of the Belt Parkway on a hot fall day about 5 P.M. amid heavy traffic. Miss Austin still didn't know exactly where the facility was located.

"Where are we going?" I asked.

"To a home."

I sat quietly observing the scenery around the bridge we were to cross. The home was located in a remote section of Staten Island. As we drove up a long winding driveway, passing trees and shrubs that neatly lined the curb, we approached the main building encircled in what seemed like a forest of trees and ivy. It had the appeal of an eighteenth-century church. The grounds were neatly kept. Four cottages were located east and west of the main house, as I later referred to it. We waited in a sitting room located in the lobby. Here we were introduced to the director of the facility and my new caseworker. I was given a brief orientation of the rules and hardly noticed Miss Austin's departure.

"Every child is on a thirty-day probationary period," the director of the facility explained. "In order to obtain a weekend pass, your group mother and social worker will decide whether or not the pass will be granted depending on your behavior."

Shortly after, the group mother of Saint Anne's, the unit within St. Michael's that I was assigned to, escorted me upstairs. My quarters were located north of the main house. I shared a room with one other girl. The setup was dormitory living. Some parts of the sleeping units were unfinished. It left something to be desired. The group mother, after showing me where I was to put my things, tried her best to comfort me.

"Don't cry, it will be all right," she said.

Not really paying attention, I looked around the room, trying to get an impression of the person with whom I would share it. Nothing in the room showed any sign of another identity, no pictures or posters, just an unmade bed, and the lingering smell of dirty laundry.

The other girls were coming in from school now. One of the girls came over and introduced herself; the others looked me over and spoke in an inquisitive manner. A girl named Beth seemed friendly, if cautious, leaving me a bit more at ease.

This co-ed facility housed two-hundred children and was an "open" facility, meaning there was freedom of movement without constant supervision. But you had to be in by your set curfew.

On the second day at "the Rock," as we referred to it,

the group mother led me around the building. The structure seemed like a maze of long halls.

"The school is located below St. Joseph's."

"What's that?" I asked.

"It's the group area for the younger boys between six and twelve years of age, still within the complex."

Already I didn't like it. After registering for classes, I looked around. The school was nothing like what I had pictured. The main office, painted a dingy green, was located on the same floor as the kitchen for the facility. When I asked for some of the same classes I had taken at Martin Van Buren, I kept hearing, "We don't offer those subjects. Only remedial studies."

I became outraged, because I was ahead in most of my studies and now I had to settle for less. Being deprived of the academic nurturing that I considered necessary, I refused to go to school. I told the group mother, "I'm not going. Is there a way I could go to an outside school?"

"You'll have to be tested first."

Pam came to my office today with me. I had met her in the group area. She came in and sat down. The worker asked her how she liked the home, she began to cry. She said she didn't like it. Pam described herself as a quiet, nervous person who likes clean places and self-respecting people. Pam feels that St. M.'s isn't the place for her. She complained of her roommate's untidiness and said she had to clean the kitchen the first day she came. Pam is a fifteen-year-old black girl with a round face and figure. She seems intelligent and verbal. Pam speaks slowly and appears to be choosing her words. Pam talks freely about her past life and doesn't attempt to make things sound better or worse, but seems capable of telling things the way they were. Pam does, however, exhibit paranoid tendencies. The worker foresees the need for a lot of supportive contact with Pam.

Pam's development history shows a real undue amount of rejection on the part of others towards Pam. Pam in return, in more recent years, has shown rejection symptoms herself. Pam at present is unable to trust. In the group area as well as in school, Pam shows that she is not able to control herself. Pam refuses to adhere to the rules set down and, if compelled to conform to such rules, she will react violently.[8]

Still nothing came of our meeting. Eventually, I lived with the situation, but not without a fight.

Pam came to the office to talk. She complained about school and she said she was learning nothing. Only dumb kids were in her class. She complained about the group and said she was sick of "wiping their asses." Pamela was crocheting with bright red thread at the time and kept making mistakes. Despite her complaining, she seemed happy.

A case conference was held on Pam. Ann A. Yankowitz briefly stated Pam's present situation, citing the possibility of placement with her aunt. Marion Crowley reported on Pam's group behavior. The question which Marion Crowley wished to have considered was placement in an outside school. Dr. Bower said that he was unsure that Pam could cope in outside school for academic as well as personal reasons. He reports that the Copiague School was contacted and that Pam had not adjusted well there. In order to keep her quiet, teachers were ordered to pass her. Marion Crowley felt that Pam should be given a chance to attend outside school. Sister Carol stated that we should take one step at a time and see how everything would work out with the aunt. Robert Ventura expressed concern that the aunt's interest might be transitory.[9]

I took up listening to gospel on a New Jersey station, collecting my thoughts, always feeling soothed by the music. I'd fall off to sleep, praying for the Lord to be merciful, to have mercy on me.

Rumor had it that the grounds supervisor, Mr. Ventura, had an unorthodox way of waking up the girls he considered defiant or hard to wake up. He would come in, sometimes two or three hours early, and dump water on the girls or turn over the bed with the girl still in it. I got the impression he enjoyed this. He was known for his outlandish behavior. With newcomers, he never knocked before entering their rooms until they set ground, which meant trying to kick his butt first by throwing objects or anything within reach to let him know they're one he can't get over on. On one occasion, he confronted Josephine, who slept in the nude. During the process of awakening her by overturning her bed, he tried to fondle her. She jumped up swinging—she slept with one eye open. Everyone was on to him and as a result I never slept in anything other than shorts and a T-shirt. One day, some of us decided to get back at this bastard, so I broke bobby pins in half and stuck them in the valves of his tires for slow leaks. He never found out why he kept getting flats.

The first weeks here passed slowly. But after the first month, life began to take shape. Saint Michael's housed children of all different ethnic and socioeconomic backgrounds. The mixture of various personalities would cause havoc. A short, muscular girl named Nicole came from the Bronx. She carried a street or gangland mentality about her. Nicole would strut about cussing anyone in her path. Her usual line was "What the fuck are you looking at?" She decided to start a clique with a circle of girls. The participants were to pay her a certain amount of their weekly allowances for dues. I tried to stay as far away from her as possible. She turned me off. The word had it that she was using these people as flunkies to do her dirty work.

Nicole called me to her room one day where she was having a meeting. I wasn't looking for trouble, but one of the girls in the clique claimed that I had been picking on her. When I entered her room, there were about five girls present. Others came later. She questioned me.

"You want to join?"

"I'll think about it." It seemed better to leave it at that, since I had no intention of joining. I wasn't giving my allowance to anyone.

Later that evening, I went upstairs to the high school group area where the older girls, from fifteen to twenty years of age, lived. From them I found out that Nicole had two of my friends, Cheryl and Renee, up at all hours of the night doing her laundry, and up early in the morning to iron and to cook her breakfast.

The dues the girls were paying turned out to be sixty percent of their allowances, which Nicole kept for her own personal use. There were times when I could hear her screaming at them for not completing a job. The girls would come to school half asleep.

Eventually, with the help of some of the counselors, the victims decided to hold a meeting with Nicole. Those who had become caught up in this mess were too afraid to speak up for fear of returning to a confrontation with Nicole's supporters. The group mother for the high school area, collaborating with the victims and their social workers, arranged for a meeting to be held in the main house, in the administration's conference room. Both the social workers and counselors were present. The tension filled the room while we awaited her entrance. Finally, she was escorted in by her social worker. I watched Nicole's expression as she entered, looking surprised, yet threatening. The proceedings began. The attending supervisor addressed her.

"We are here to find out what the problems are with you and the other girls."

Quickly she responded, "There's no problem," while rolling her eyes, with the intention of intimidating those present. She denied everything in spite of the fact that others were there. Renee became so scared she ran out of the room crying. She knew Nicole would try and get back at her. The meeting turned into a shouting match. I kept quiet and observed.

Once we returned to our group areas, things were too quiet and the tensions were high. That evening I walked upstairs where I found Cheryl and Loretta in the T.V. room talking about what had taken place earlier. Loretta was trying hard to comfort Cheryl, letting her know that she didn't have to be afraid. Nicole kept calling out for Cheryl and Loretta, but the other girls would not allow them to respond. They felt that if she wanted them, she would have to come and get them. I was astounded when the girls stood up to Nicole. Nicole had no choice but to stop intimidating the others. Later on, this girl who had tried to victimize her peers would herself become a victim of drug abuse and degradation in her relations with men.

One day, Nicole convinced Cheryl and me to 'break night,' which meant staying up and out all night. Going along, we travelled by subway to Manhattan to her boyfriend's house. From the outside, no one would have believed anyone lived in that tenement—windows boarded up, the steps deteriorating. When we entered the apartment, there sat an older woman at the kitchen table. Shaking like leaves, we were asked to sit down. I couldn't. Cheryl had to use the bathroom. After looking over the place I whispered to Cheryl, "Don't use the bathroom here. I think you'd better wait."

Finally, Nicole's boyfriend walked in. Having heard about the telltale signs of drug users, I immediately noticed the swelling of his hands. He took us outside to a van and we proceeded to ride around all night long. Only after we reached White Castle, somewhere in the Bronx, did a feeling come across me that something wasn't right. I still believe the van was stolen. When we reached the home that morning about 6 A.M., I had never been so glad to know that I had someplace to call home. We all showered and went to school as if nothing had happened—although we'd had an experience I'll never forget. Eighteen days later I had a visitor.

Pam has had little or no contact with her family since she was six years old. Her family info is scanty. Her father's whereabouts are unknown.

Her aunt Mrs. Wittaker, arrived today. She was a neatly dressed, black woman about 5'7" in height. Mrs. Wittaker came to the worker's office, where the worker told Mrs. Wittaker about Pam's talent and high intelligence and the worker also told Mrs. Wittaker about Pam's emotional instability. Mrs. Wittaker listened to all the worker had to say and explained that taking Pam into her home would not be the same as taking any ordinary child. Mrs. Wittaker said that she understood and said that her sister (Pam's mother) had been much like Pam. She added that she wanted Pam and believed that she could handle any difficulties. The worker asked then if she would like to meet Pam and she responded "Yes."[10]

I received a phone call from my social worker summoning me to her office. As I walked in, I was introduced to an aunt whom I never knew existed until this time.

Pam seemed shy and slightly resistive. Mrs. Wittaker was beaming with enthusiasm. Pam, for the first few minutes, was quite rude to both her aunt and the worker. Her aunt seemed to know how to handle the situation and Pam soon became quite pleasant. Her aunt had brought some pictures of Pam as a baby. She passed them around to the workers and Pam. Pam didn't look at the pictures long. She seemed confused and almost seemed to be wondering what she should do next. The worker offered Mrs. Wittaker a soda. Mr. Brown, the supervisor, was present. He asked Mrs. Wittaker, "Would you like some brownies that Pam just made to go along with the soda?" Meanwhile, Pam ran upstairs to get her crocheting to show to her aunt. The worker later met Mrs. Wittaker and Pam at the bus stop as she was leaving work. Mrs. Wittaker said that they had a very nice visit. Pam seemed very happy. The worker and Mrs. Wittaker got on the bus together after Pam and her aunt embraced and said goodbye. During the 45-minute bus ride to the ferry, Mrs. Wittaker told the worker that she had taken care of Pam and her sister when they were young since Pam's mother was unable to do so. She did this until Pam was about three and a half and then Pam's mother told her that she was trying to steal her children from her. She wouldn't allow the aunt to see the children anymore. The aunt also stated that she had heard of Pam through the father who lied and told her that Pam was with him. When she found out that Pam was institutionalized, she attempted to visit her. For some reason, she was not allowed to visit at the hospital when she arrived there.[11]

My aunt and the social worker had discussed arrangements for me to visit her during Thanksgiving. I made that visit to Philadelphia where, for the first time since I was four, I would have a meal with blood relatives. I met my cousin whom I got along with right from the start. During my stay, questions were asked about my life before entering St. Michael's such as what activities I enjoyed. My reluctance to answer many of the questions sprang partly from the anger that was building in me. Why, out of all the children born in the family, was I the only child forgotten for so long? I would have been willing to live with my cousin had that option been available but my aunt wanted me to live with her. Dissension between the two of them allowed no peace; therefore I declined, saying I didn't care much for Philly. My aunt brought to my attention that the family's hands were tied all those years.

"Your father, when signing you over to the State, stipulated that none of my family members were to get custody of you. I made an attempt to visit you when I lived in New York. When I reached Rockland County, I tried to see you but they wouldn't allow me to. I left you a doll." I just looked at her as though I knew about it. In reality, I never received the doll or heard anything about her visit six years ago before now.

"When you were a little girl," continued my aunt, "I'd travel back and forth from work to your mother's just to change you and make sure you had at least one good meal a day. On occasion, I found your mother knocked out, stone drunk. We would get into arguments over you. She didn't want anyone to do anything for you or your sister."

"I had a sister?"

"Yes. You probably don't remember. Her name was Carolyn. She died in 1968 of water on the brain. She was one year younger than you. One time, I witnessed you standing on a chair over the sink trying to give her something to drink and you were no more than a baby yourself." Trying to hold back any sign of emotion, my eyes still began to tear.

After my return to New York, the social worker approached me with the idea of living with my aunt. I refused the offer, partly because I didn't feel that her living quarters in Philly were large enough for the both of us and also I did feel a bit resentful, thinking, *why now? Where were you when I needed you nine years ago?* Besides, I was tired of being bounced from one place to another and I had freedom now. I had already been molded into what I wanted to be and my direction was good.

For Christmas, I visited Washington, D.C. and met the rest of the family at my grandmother's home. It seemed that they observed me very closely and so I became very withdrawn. They expected that, because through the grapevine other relatives had stated that I behaved in an antisocial way during the visit to my aunt's in Philadelphia in November. It became a no-win situation. Everything I said became null and void.

I wanted this visit to be over earlier than planned, so that I could get back to New York to wash clothes and then be off to Long Island for New Year's Eve at the Harrises, which was just better than being alone. When it came time for my departure from Washington, my family seemed concerned as to why I wasn't staying for the entire Christmas vacation. I felt very uncomfortable. They had no idea what my plans were and I wasn't going to tell them. It would have only made matters worse. I really didn't have a sense of belonging, I knew very little about them and they only knew me from what had been told to them by the social worker, which was one-sided.

> Mrs. Wittaker called to say that she had received a letter from Pam stating that she didn't want to come to live with her. The worker explored with Mrs. Wittaker how she felt about it. She said she'd be only too happy to have her but would not force her and that the same holds true for the grandmother.[12]

A week after I returned to St. Michael's, I received a disturbing letter from another aunt who had been visiting Washington while I was there. Her letter said that I had used the family and acted antisocially towards them. I credited her thoughts to her own guilt for not showing any great concern before now. From that day on, I didn't encourage contact because they had already passed judgment, and still today, we're on shaky ground. I'm not regarded as a family member; I became the victim of *their* circumstances not of my own. I didn't place myself as a ward of the State, my father did. I believe if the family really wanted me, no court in the United States would have denied them that right as long as they were fit guardians.

> On 9/26/73, the staff psychiatrist noted "One is particularly struck by her sensitivity, low self-esteem and vulnerability to loss and to 'adverse' circumstances, as well as her tremendous all-inclusive anger." Her anger and thinking is dominated by her hurt feelings, but is normal as far as clarity, logic and coherence are concerned. Her goals are clearly expressed. Her intelligence appears average or above." On 2/74 he stated, "she requested an opportunity to be considered for foster home placement." It appears that it would be worthwhile to consider placement. At Euphrasian her I.Q. was found to be in the bright-normal range (110–119). Her academic achievement is somewhat behind her mental ability. The recommendation stated "at present, there is no evidence of psychotic decompensation." Contact between Pam and her mother's family has slackened off although both her grandmother and her uncle continue to write.[13]

After the first three months, time seemed to speed up. By spring time I felt in tune with the pace of life at

St. Michael's. Things were normal considering "normal" always included something bizarre going on. For example, Marcy (a resident we knew as "Dangerbrain") had two rookie counselors barricaded in a counselor's room at about one o'clock in the morning. They were horrified because they had been told that she was disturbed. She had been requesting something of them and had somehow talked her way into the counselor's area, where no residents were allowed. By the time the evening supervisors came to aid them, the counselors were outside on the window ledge. This was just one of many antics in the life of St. Michael's.

It was difficult for each of us at "the Rock," living in close quarters with little privacy, adjusting to life without a real family or a real home. Some of the counselors should be commended for their efforts to make life easier. I had a knack for cooking. Usually, the food was sent to the floor already prepared. The counselors were able to get authorization to have the food sent up uncooked, so I could cook for my group area.

I also enjoyed sewing, something I picked up years earlier at my friend Kena's house. Nellie Holmes, a group mother, owned a sewing shop in New Jersey, and on occasion would take me there when I wanted to make something to wear. She would help me complete the garments. Through her, we were able to obtain a sewing machine for use by others who wanted to learn the skill.

Bessie, the night counselor, became the grandmother

of the 11 P.M. to 7 A.M. shift. She would always come in cheerful. You would find her doing someone's hair. We all treated her with the greatest respect, and for those who didn't, one of us would let them know about it. This included the boys from the cottages, who showed her respect as well.

Cheryl, Carolyn and I had all sung in the choir as children, and the counselors we maintained relationships with, who also tended to carry strong religious beliefs, would encourage our love of singing. Usually we would get together and create dance routines among ourselves to the tunes of the Isley Brothers and Earth, Wind and Fire, which were our favorite groups. Carolyn decided that we should form our own group. I would make outfits for the performances. We would enter amateur night at the Apollo. Carolyn, having spent the last several years in Harlem before coming to St. M.'s, believed that she could find a sponsor for us. I discouraged this idea, and preferred to continue with our back room singing. We did do exceptional harmony and the counselors enjoyed our voices.

Then one of the administrators asked if we would sing at the chapel on the grounds for a program designed to encourage all the residents to attend church services. Church attendance was unusual for most of us. I had not been inside a church now for more than two years. It was a refreshing change. Everyone gathered in the chapel to see Carolyn, Cheryl and I sing "Lean On Me" by Bill Withers. I was nervous standing in front of so many people and wanted to back out, but I drummed up enough courage to follow it through. When we finished the song, everyone applauded and tears came to our eyes. The important thing for me was the spirit that flowed through the chapel that day.

Carolyn wanted our group more than ever to go to the Apollo. Mr. Morris, one of the supervisors in Administration, shared Carolyn's excitement and offered to sponsor us and to provide anything I needed to make our costumes. But I declined, and Cheryl and Carolyn didn't want to do it if we weren't going to do it together. I was too self-conscious to stand on a stage in a theater to be booed down and I just knew that the crowd at the Apollo would have a field day with us. So we just left it to thought, and thought was all it was.

The turnover in staff at St. Michael's was continuous, perhaps in part due to the behavior of some of the residents. In some cases, new counselors were blatant in refusing to interact with the residents; refusing, for instance, to take us shopping or to the movies. One of the most uncomfortable situations occurred whenever we went shopping for clothes. We usually went in groups of about five. The store clerks treated us like diseased people, whispering with a watchful eye. Although we were accompanied by a counselor, some of the girls were sometimes caught stealing. This was partly the result of having limited funds for clothing. The allotment ranged around $138 per child per year. Meanwhile, fashion dictated that we keep up with the times, so the girls would steal.

Confrontations with the counselors, or between residents, were usually verbal, unless the individual felt she was being provoked. There was an incident when a small thirteen-year-old girl from the high school group area, also named Carolyn like my friend, went into an area adjacent to St. Anne's to borrow something. She found herself in a throwdown with Jeri, who was sixteen, weighed about 160 pounds and was approximately five feet six inches tall. They knocked down the bookshelf that was standing against the wall. The sound of the shelf falling drew the attention of everyone within the area. When Bob, one of the male counselors on duty, came in to break it up, he found himself entangled in the mess. All of a sudden, I saw Carolyn lock both her hands and swing. She made contact with Bob's eye and broke his contact lens. It was like something out of a movie to see a thirteen-year-old girl with such coordination and strength.

The counselor understood he was in the wrong place at the wrong time. Once Carolyn realized what she had done, she tried very hard to console Bob. Holding his head in his hands, he kept telling her that it was O.K., that he knew that that blow wasn't meant for him. He later became our hero of sorts.

I was no goody two-shoes either. A couple of girls and I would play hookey from the Mickey Mouse school on Fridays and steal our group area's allowance, which the group mother had picked up early in the day. Since the group areas were unfinished, we would climb over the partitions and bend back the thin, pressed wood door keeping the lock still in place and someone would slide the money envelope out. We would then divide it up and eat to our hearts content.

On one occasion, I requested a visit to my grand-mother and the social worker, Ms. Mary Anne, denied the request with no explanation. I threw a tantrum in the office and it carried over into the recreation room located in St. Anne's. But her decision held firm. A few hours later, I tried her again, this time requesting a visit to the Harrises for the weekend.

> Later, Pam returned. She told the worker that she wanted to go to the Harris's. She wanted to call the Harrises. The worker said that it was a long distance phone call. She told the worker that it wasn't coming out of her pocket so to shut up and make the call.[14]

Finally, my wish was granted so that I was allowed to visit the Harrises. Eventually they allowed me to visit the Harrises on a regular basis, whenever I felt the need to get away from the dormitory lifestyle.

After Pete and I left, the Harrises changed child care agencies and now were housing children who were much younger. They had Lucille who was two years of age and her brother, four. Through my visits, Lucille and I had grown attached to one another. She'd look forward to my cornrowing her hair and I would just enjoy having someone to care for. I wanted to give to those children who, like me, were lacking stability in their lives. After I completed braiding her hair, Lucille would prance around the house, full of smiles. She loved Papa as all the kids before her had. At times, he'd have as many as three on his lap; some would fight just to get near enough to him to be tickled. He knew of a ticklish spot right around the knees that never failed.

Sometimes, cutting my visit short, I would leave on Saturday instead of Sunday. Papa always offered to drive me to the train station. Lucille would come for the ride. She'd cry sometimes that I was leaving and, feeling a bit uneasy, I decided not to visit as often to avoid seeing her cry. Papa and I would always talk on our way into the village, carrying on our own private conversation during this brief time: He'd let me know what was going on in the house, things that no one else would share with me, like how the children were doing in school and some background history of the children they cared for now. Papa was always willing to listen to my aspirations. I'd let him know about school and what my plans were for the future: things I had long dreamed of having and wanted to accomplish on my own.

"Papa, one day I'd like a car and an apartment of my own. I know I'll have to work at it."

He just nodded his head. "You'll get it if you stick to

it." Before departing, he'd ask, "When will you be returning?"

I'd look into his eyes, not yet knowing when and reply, "The train is coming, I'll see you soon."

> Foster home placement has been initiated through Open Door, Mrs. Lomax, at Division for Youth. It would appear that such placement is warranted and has a good chance of meeting success. On July 15, 1974, Pam was scheduled to be transferred to a foster home. On the evening of July 11th, Pam ran wild through the groups. She conducted a "reign of terror." Pam totally lost control. She struck two childcare workers with the aid of another resident. Childcare feared for the safety of the group and admitted both Pam and the other resident to the M.P.U. 24-hour room. Pam left for her foster home from the M.P.U.[15]

Finally, after ten months of requesting removal from that hellhole and test placements in two other foster homes that didn't work out, the Division of Youth worker found a foster home in Ozone Park, Queens. This would be the fifth in my lifetime and the last. By this point, I had given up on living a normal life.

Then, four days before I was to leave, something happened. They called it a "reign of terror." I call it a panic attack. One month away from my sixteenth birthday, I suddenly felt that I had no future, that my life was a dead end and that there was nothing I could do about it. The best response I could muster was to try and convince myself that I just didn't care what happened to me. That evening I walked down the halls with another girl who must have felt the same way, breaking things and hitting anyone who tried to stop us. They still let me try the foster home placement, but I think it was only to get rid of me.

Mrs. Dorsey, a stout woman about fifty years of age, with a demanding tone of voice, lived in a brick two-family house with two irritating long-haired chihuahuas that would attack if you so much as sneezed.

To my surprise, Mrs. Dorsey also cared for the son of Linda, the girl, now a woman, from the Jackson's, the foster home where I had previously lived. The baby was about two years old. I didn't see much of Linda. I didn't feel comfortable with the setup and I definitely wanted to avoid Linda at all costs. According to Mrs. Dorsey, Linda had turned out to be an irresponsible parent and Mrs. Dorsey, who had been another of Linda's former foster mothers, was attempting to acquire custody of the little boy.

Luckily, this placement was considered a test. On the third day, before I turned in for the night, a feeling came over me that something was going to happen that was being kept from me. As I closed my eyes, I remembered the day I was taken to Queens Children's. The strange thing was that Mrs. Dorsey and I had said very little to one another all day.

The next morning she called me down for breakfast. Still we said barely anything to each other beyond a casual greeting. At about 10:30 A.M., a social worker drove up in a black car. The feeling of fear intensified. It seemed like a bad dream repeating itself. The style and the color of the car took me back to the day when I was taken to Queens Children's. I was frightened and had the idea I definitely didn't want to return there. The worker helped me with my bags. Without a word being said, we started back to St. Michael's, or so I believed.

> The Division contacted St. M.'s and requested that Pam be removed from the home. Plans were made to have Pam admitted to Elmhurst General Psychiatric ward directly from the foster home. However, Pam was transported back to St. M.'s from where the worker escorted her immediately to Elmhurst General. Pam vowed she'd "make a fool" out of the worker by proving that she did not need hospitalization. After three wks. at the hospital, it was concluded that she was reintegrated and could return to group living. St. M.'s does not feel that we can meet Pam's needs and is seeking further hospitalization.[16]

Once again I was ushered into the hellish world of the tenth floor—the mental ward. Only now, at sixteen a little wiser, I could better handle the zombies and the other dangers. I knew what was expected of me, and how to keep to myself. After three weeks I returned to St. M.'s like a battle-weary soldier, heavily under the effects of the mood-altering medication, Stellazine. There, over the next two months, I recovered my strength.

But in the third week of October, I had another rude awakening. The word had circulated quickly, through a slip of the tongue by a counselor returning from a staff meeting, that I was to be placed in the M.P.U. (Multi-Purpose Unit). Cheryl had confided in a counselor close to her about the plans of the social worker to have me put into the M.P.U. The counselors on duty in the group area at the time confronted me, asking, "Do you want to leave, Pam?"

"I have nowhere to go." I answered.

"Why don't you go to Philly to your aunt's? Don't worry, we'll give you the carfare. How much is it?"

"Fifteen dollars round trip."

The counselors scrambled through their pockets, pooling together enough money to get me there, hoping to save me from the M.P.U. encounter. So I got the bus an hour later, slipping out with the help of my friends.

The staff consulted and concluded that the M.P.U. placement was necessary. It was planned to place Pam in the M.P.U. on October 22nd. This plan was altered as the entire girls' side is in a state of turmoil. Pam absconded on the 24th and turned up in Philadelphia at her aunt's. Mrs. Wit-

taker notified St. Michael's and on the 27th she
put Pam on the bus back to St. Michael's. Mrs.
Wittaker is extremely distressed.[17]

Upon my return, I told Cheryl what had happened,
that my aunt said I couldn't stay there. Although she
was my best and most trusted friend, even Cheryl was
at a loss what to suggest. For the moment, the order to
place me in the M.P.U. had been put on hold, so I was
allowed to return to my group area. But that was no
permanent solution. The counselors who had assisted
me and cared were still concerned about what I was
going to do.

"I can't go back to Philly. She'd only send me back
again, and it makes no sense to run."

CHAPTER 5

THE M. P. U. UNIT

Only two days later, on October 29, 1974, I awakened with the realization that an entire year had passed. At sixteen I had served thirteen months here at St. Michael's and survived. My day started off well considering that, as usual, my sleep had been interrupted several times during the night. There were always some residents who were 'breaking night'—pulling fire alarms or setting the garbage dumpsters ablaze. Worse was being awakened to find three or four girls standing over your bed ready to rip you to shreds based on hearsay. Occurrences like this were not uncommon in large facilities like St. M.'s. There was no telling when your slumber would be broken by another's sudden expression of outrage.

The morning was grey, clouded, as I stood on the roof of the high school group area overlooking the grounds. I had a view of the chapel directly below me, and of the parking lot to my left by the main road, which led to a world outside the one I had now to conform to. The gate house, or parsonage, where the priest lived, was to my right beside the tree-lined drive-way. Everything was calm as I surveyed the scene before me. But that was about to change, radically. Just a few minutes earlier, I had gone upstairs to visit with Renee and Cheryl. Leaving their floor, I opened the door that led to the stairwell where Jenny was talking on the pay phone, just as Jenny hung up. She turned and nudged me as if to say "get out of my way." Jenny and I had a tendency to get under one another's skin. We couldn't stand each other and all I needed was an excuse. Needless to say, a fight ensued. We scuffled back and forth on the very narrow landing of the stairway. When one of the counselors came to break it up, Jenny claimed that I had tried to knock her down the stairs. By mid-day, my newly assigned social worker, Doris, the fifth to enter my life and the second I'd had here at St. Michael's had, without my knowledge, checked me into the M.P.U.

I received a call stating that I was to go see Dr. Bloomberg. As I turned around after hanging up the phone, I discovered that they had sent Jack, the Bruiser, and one other counselor from the unit. I went along peacefully and without restraints. Word had it that Jack was worse than Mr. Ventura when it came to manhandling the girls.

The M.P.U. was known among the residents as the place to stay away from. It was a world within a world, set apart from the mainstream of the facility. The residents of the M.P.U. were rarely seen outside of the unit, prohibited from socializing on the grounds, always under lock and key. I had landed myself behind the walls of doom.

Dr. Bloomberg, the head physician, placed me directly in confinement. I was given a briefing on how the unit was run and what was expected of me. Under their point system, I was to attend school, take prescribed medication and do assigned chores. Chores? The stench of garbage that lingered in the tightly closed building suggested that very few of the residents did chores. No one was allowed off the grounds without a counselor. You worked up the levels of the ladder from D to A (discharge level).

Levels D and C were the worst, where you did nothing outside the walls of the M.P.U. Outside contact with my friends occurred only during classes. Even during lunch, when everyone reported back to their group areas, those from the M.P.U. were restricted to the M.P.U.

The small complex housed six to eight residents, all girls. Only rarely were boys ever placed here, which was surprising since St. Michael's housed boys and girls in roughly equal numbers. Like the rest of the facility, the unit operated on three shifts around the clock. The staff consisted of two counselors per shift and one nurse to administer medication. Jack, the Bruiser, would double as the nurse when needed as well as Staff Supervisor. Again I was placed on Stellazine twice a day at 50 milligrams. When Jack was on duty I had no choice but to swallow my dosage. The rest of the time, I had ways to avoid having to ingest this mess without the nurse or the counselor knowing. As soon as they turned their backs, I'd spit the medicine out on the rug or make a quick exit towards the bathroom.

> Pam is reacting poorly to the behavior modification program employed at the M.P.U. She is not interacting with the members and considers herself far superior. At this time, she acts as another counselor, reports on the members and advises staff how to act. She maintains contact with her friends—both in school and on unplanned group visits. Pam is attempting to manipulate M.P.U. staff members who are aware of her games. She is learning the channels of command and, as in the past, goes to the 'head man' to complain.[18]

The faces here at the M.P.U. were new to me. Two residents, Rhonda and Regina were kept heavily sedated, and slept for most of the day. A third resident, "Danger Brain," had spent some time in the unit's twenty-four-hour room for setting fire to the garbage in St. Ann's group area. Then there was Tee Tee, who was about 8 years of age, a small-framed girl sent over from the younger girls' group area, St. Theresa's, for fighting with another resident. Others would come and go according to the whims of the staff. The M.P.U. was also used as a holding pen for residents the staff felt might go out of control unpredictably. I had very little interaction with people here except for the psychologist, Ben Driscoll, whom I saw on a weekly basis. In his office, he would ask me how I felt about being here. At first, I'd stare at him as though I could see through him. Only after a long interval of silence would I speak.

"I don't like being here."

"Do you want to play the games displayed on the table?"

"No," I said, looking at him as though *he* needed therapy.

The staring went on for weeks at each 45-minute session until finally I decided to ask him, "Don't you think that these sessions are a bit boring? Really, you're not getting anywhere, so why continue? You're still getting paid, so why waste my time and yours? I'm sick and damn tired of being picked at and probed by you. Why would I need to express myself to you? For what? So you can have me committed?"

In the early days of January, 1975, the unit was moved to new quarters, due to the appalling condition of the old ones. The staff was undergoing a complete makeover as well. Dr. Driscoll stayed on but the head physician for the unit, Dr. Bloomberg, was being replaced by Dr. Madison. Rhonda was overjoyed as though she had just seen Santa Claus since she didn't care for Dr. Bloomberg.

Dr. Madison, a tall, well-spoken man was, to my surprise, compassionate compared to the previous physicians. Coming from a facility in Florida, he noticed discrepancies in how things were run here and decided to make some alterations. He was heaven sent in my eyes. I found him willing to listen without jumping to conclusions; I felt comfortable in expressing myself to him, describing my situation, and protesting the poor quality of education offered at the home, without feeling that what I had to say would get back to those at the main house. With Dr. Madison in charge, life at the M.P.U. had a chance. Not only did he keep our conversations confidential, he fought very hard to improve the way I was perceived by others.

> Pam is adjusting well to the new rules and regulations of the unit. She is manipulating some of the rules, so that she can see her friends in the group. She is not openly violating these rules. The team is aware and will confront her with the recognition of manipulation. Pam has been doing a great deal of cooking which is enjoyed by staff and group alike. Pam has lost a great deal of weight and is concerned about her appearance and hygiene. Pam has maintained herself on 'A' level.[19]

The M.P.U. was a circus at times. Throughout the spring, I tried to keep my spirits up by doing what came naturally to me—cooking. John and Mel, the staff on the night shift, encouraged me by bringing in chicken and steaks for me to prepare and the three of us often shared them while the others slept. John and Mel spoiled me to death with flattery and that was all right with me. I enjoyed their company and soon I got to know their families. The facility had a rule that staff members weren't allowed to let the residents become involved in their personal lives. But John and Mel broke the rule, not just with me but with others as well, and this added to our sense of belonging and enhanced our understanding of people. John and Mel didn't see us as outcasts, but as children who were abandoned and needed guidance.

For Memorial Day, I decided to cook a meal for the unit. The menu was to be fried chicken, macaroni salad and ribs; one counselor requested greens; and I wanted peach cobbler. For the occasion, all the counselors on the 3 to 11 shift pitched in with groceries and the counselors on the 11 to 7 shift agreed to come in early so that everyone would be eating together. That morning one of the counselors had taken me out to the mall for last minute items and to browse. I fell in love with a poster of a lion—my astrological sign being Leo—but I didn't have enough money on me to buy it. I had spent all I had on pie crust mix for the peach cobbler. Leaving the poster behind, we started back to St. M.'s so I could prepare the meal. The counselors really got into the right spirit. Even the Bruiser chipped in with sodas—so what if they were warm and there was no ice in the freezer to cool them. Julio, one of the 3 to 11 shift counselors, went out to get ice. Just as I completed the meal, Julio returned with the ice. We were ready to eat.

When my friends from the main house, Cheryl and Renee, learned that I had cooked, they requested permission to join in and arrived just in time. Just as I put the sodas on the table, Julio pulled out the poster I had admired earlier in the day from beside the refrigerator. When I spotted it, I screamed with excitement!

"Is that for me? Thank you. You had it framed." Now I knew why it took him so long to get the ice.

The M.P.U. wasn't *all* fun and games. One day I was in my room when I heard Rhonda and the day counselor, Phil, arguing. I came out into the hall to see what was going on. Phil was standing at Rhonda's bedroom door, trying to persuade her to open the door and leave her room since she had a lit cigarette, which was against the rules. I tried to talk with Rhonda. Meanwhile, Phil went downstairs to get the other counselor, Sam, to assist him. They returned to the floor and found me in Rhonda's room talking with her. Rhonda had taken the dresser and pushed it in front of the door. When the counselors were able to open the door, I was told to leave. By the time I reached the dining area, I had lit a cigarette. At that moment, Sam came running down the stairs and slapped the cigarette out of my mouth.

"What is your problem?" I asked. "I didn't have anything to do with Rhonda and you can ask Phil."

Sam carried on in the authoritative tone of a senior child-care worker, then he pushed me. I refused to just stand there. A fight ensued during which I punched him in the face.

Dragging me down the stairs leading from the dining area, Sam shouted, "That's it! You're going to the blue room."

Fighting with all my strength, I was thrown into a room padded in blue. "I'm not staying in here, you fuck!"

"We'll see!"

"Oh, yeah?"

Kicking with all my will, I knocked the door completely off its hinges. Sam ran back down the stairs, enraged.

"That's it! Get upstairs to your room!" he screamed.

"No! I'll be damned if I'm going to be punished for something I didn't do!"

"You're going to your room!" he yelled, pushing me again.

Struggling with all my might, I fought him all the way to my room, objects in our path falling left and right. Sam punched me in the eye. I held on as he swung, the impact throwing us over the bed. Before I knew it, the grounds supervisor from the main house had made his way to East Cottage, supposedly to aid Sam. Well, he brought company. Cheryl, Carolyn and a few others were right behind the supervisor. Carolyn, pregnant at the time, flew into a rage when she spotted me on the floor with blood running from my mouth and my eye blackened. There was a free-for-all. In the condition I was in I can't even say how long it lasted.

Finally, things calmed down. Sam talked to me from the door. "You know, from now on you're on Level D with no privileges."

Having to work my way back up to Level A would probably just make things worse, but I had no choice but to go along. The following Monday, Jack, the unit supervisor for the M.P.U., came in early just to get the details of the weekend incident. He called me down to his office. "Pam, what happened?" he asked.

I told him my side of the story and pointed out what made my pride hurt so much more than my blackened eye. "Do I have to stay on Level D? It's not fair. I don't know what was wrong with Sam, I was just trying to help."

"Well, now you know what being victimized is all about," he said.

"Can I speak with Dr. Madison?"

"What do you want to tell him?"

"The same thing I told you."

"I'll relay the message to him at the staff meeting." He paused, then continued, "But I think you will still have to work your way back to Level A."

Pam and a few other residents became involved in a physical confrontation with staff. She totally lost control, many attempts were made to calm her down but none were successful except for physical restraint. Pam was scratched and received a bruise under her left eye. She perceives this incident as an injustice since staff hit first.[20]

I couldn't stand it. Constantly under supervision, with no room to breathe, still raging inside against Sam. When he'd come on duty, I wouldn't look him in the face; I'd just growl. Dr. Madison called me down to the old M.P.U., now used as the administrative offices for the unit. We discussed the matter and he placed me on Level B as a compromise.

"Oh, Pam, by the way, I was able to obtain funds from the Administration for you to take the course you wanted at Baruch College."

"Oh, really? Thank you."

Around the time of my seventeenth birthday in late August of 1975, I signed up for the Bookkeeping and Small Business Management course. During the next year I attended classes at night from 6 to 10, two nights a week, and attended high school during the day, completing the business course in the spring of 1976, a month before the school year concluded. I longed for commencement day and the chance for a life in the outside world that would follow once I was discharged from St. Michael's.

Picking up my Bookkeeping and Small Business Management certificate unaccompanied, this long-awaited dream seemed suddenly much closer, almost within reach. I experienced the thrill of accomplishment, knowing I had proven the others wrong. When I returned to the Rock the next day, I ran all through the main house, waving my piece of paper.

> Pam's grandmother is entering a senior citizen complex and is unable to plan for her. There is no relative interested in planning for her future or caring for Pam. Any contact with relatives has ceased, they show no interest in visiting.
>
> On 5/7, an Ed. conference was held. It was again stated that Pam is enrolled in the 11th grade, must attend summer school and P.S. 25 until June 1977 to graduate. Dr. Madison stated that if Pam were employed, a waiver could be requested of Albany. Pam has successfully completed the course at Baruch.[21]

As bad as my behavior at the M.P.U. had been at times, it was considered mild compared to some of the other residents of the unit. One girl, Monica, would prance around in the sheerest lingerie she could find, attempting to seduce anyone who paid any attention. John, the counselor on duty that night, said, "Why don't you talk to her? She's always calling me into her room and when I go to the door, she's lying spread-eagled on the bed."

I pulled Monica aside to let her know that she was making the counselors feel uncomfortable: "Look, I don't know what your problem is, but I think you better lay off."

"Yeah, O.K."

"Don't you have something else you can put on? I don't want John and Mel to resign because of your behavior."

Then they placed her on Valium. This accomplished nothing. It only made things worse, because then Monica stayed up all night and slept all day. Next they decided to restrict her to her room. I didn't care, as long as she stayed out of my face.

> Pam does not relate to her peer group. Monica T. and Regina R. are the only cottage members with whom Pam interacts and she tends to assume the role of an older sister giving advice on life.[22]

Every time I returned to St. Michael's after I'd been away on a weekend pass, there were new faces. That was normal—a few of the residents would go, a few new ones would take their places. But for most of us, this was the closest thing to home. In getting to know each person, I learned new things about myself. One resident in particular was able to bring up something within me that I was unaware existed. Percy was in his early teens when he entered St. Michael's in the early summer of 1976. Before coming to New York, he had been living with his family in California. As a small child, he had been a drug runner for members of his family, who were dealers. His adolescence had just been more of the same or worse. He wasn't exactly heading for an ivy league college.

With us all living in close quarters, it was easy to know what the others were about. I was still seventeen years of age. Normally, I wouldn't involve myself with the younger residents but Percy was different. He carried a strong sense of bitterness which, for me, was easy to relate to. I believed he needed someone other than an authority figure, someone who would be there to listen and understand him as a person. Percy talked to me and kept on talking to me. He described witnessing the death of his mother: shot and killed in a drug deal. He told me how, shortly afterwards, he and his brother came to New York and settled in the Bronx in a neighborhood where drugs were everybody's best friend until they became your worst enemy. Only thirteen years old, Percy was a hard-core street kid.

Like his brother, Percy was Muslim, with an abiding faith in the Islamic culture of the Five Percenters. The strongest Islamic communities at that time were among young black males generally, among prison populations in particular and in poverty-stricken neighborhoods. Islamic law forbids eating pork or any foods containing pork by-products such as lard, it requires the observance of strict hygiene, and it permits having more than one queen or wife.

Percy, a well-dressed and conscientious teen, loved the girls. As a practicing Muslim, he strongly disliked whites. Knowing this, the counselors still placed Percy in a local school outside the facility at a time when racial tension was at its peak. It was when Percy had failed and was then forced inside the school annex of St. Michael's that we met. Why, in heaven's name, had they placed him in a white community? That level of insensitivity is commonplace in institutions that warehouse unwanted children.

One day, shortly after he started school, Percy took a stroll down the deserted corridors while classes were in session to visit one of the younger children that he had taken a liking to. Percy claimed he was only returning the boy's hat, which he had dropped in the hallway. But somehow Percy's presence was mistaken to be a willful disruption of the class. The teacher reacted and there was a physical confrontation. The teacher pressed charges against Percy; the Agency was all for it. When the police arrived to take statements, the main house was a circus. Once Percy's admirers heard that he was going to be arrested, they rallied on his behalf. Some taunted the teacher, shouting obscenities and even threatening her life. They were hoping she could be frightened into dropping the charges. But in the end none of this did Percy any good. He was taken to a juvenile detention hall to await his day in court three weeks later.

When that day came three of us made sure to be at the local family court at the appointed hour to await Percy's arrival. No one from St. Michael's knew we had come, so we stayed close to the entrance of the holding pen in the courthouse to avoid being spotted by any of the staff appearing on behalf of the home. Percy arrived and we were able to speak with him as he waited to be called, but he seemed very withdrawn. I asked the counselor from the Spofford juvenile facility, Mr. Johnson, who had accompanied Percy to court, about Percy's behavior during his stay. He gave me the impression that Percy kept to himself for the most part, and assured me that Percy didn't make any trouble with the other inmates. Finally, Percy was called upstairs. We waited and waited. When Percy came back down we were told that he had been remanded back to Spofford for observation.

> Pam has become very involved with Percy in that she strongly identifies with his problems. She has chosen to be his advocate and has gone to Mr. Samuel and to fam. court in his behalf. She is on the verge of a major setback as a result of this symbiotic identification. Pam is reverting to manipulation.[23]

During his thirty-day stay at Spofford, I joined with an outside acquaintance named Asia, the cousin of one of the residents of St. Michael's, in concocting a plan to visit Percy at the juvenile facility. We hoped to get in to see him, or at least speak to the social worker assigned to his case. We agreed that I would pose as his mother and Asia as his aunt. Fully satisfied with this completely improbable little plan, we ventured off to Spofford, the juvenile prison in the Bronx, one warm summer day in mid-July. I knew very little about the inner city. Asia, who did, led the way by subway, the IRT #2. Two hours after leaving, we arrived and entered through the visitors' gate. Only two visitors per person, the guard stated. We went past the guard. My heart started to pound. We signed in as planned, then were told to wait, and we did, for about ten minutes. A man sitting beside us began to tell us about his son who was being detained here on charges of petty theft. Meanwhile, we prayed that the Administration wouldn't check or question our signatures. Well, they didn't. We watched Percy coming down the hall. Spotting us, he just smiled. Percy was glad to see us. Perhaps he knew how deeply I shared with him the loneliness you feel when there is no one that cares about you enough to do anything to help. We asked him so many questions. "How are you feeling? How are you being treated?"

"O.K. They serve pork a lot here, so I don't eat much." He did look thin and drained. Pork is cheap food, so it's regularly served in institutions, even to people whose religion prohibits it. "My brother was here once," he said a few minutes later. I wondered what it meant to him that before him his brother had been put through some of the same trials and tribulations.

I then asked if he had seen his social worker.

"I have not seen him yet."

As Percy started on his way back to his quarters, I reminded him that he must continue to show self control and present himself in a positive light towards the staff and other residents at Spofford. In response he looked back over his shoulder and gave us the thumbs-up sign, even though he was no longer smiling. We requested to see his social worker and our request was granted. As soon as Asia and I entered the office, I felt a lump in my throat, but I kept my composure. The social worker told us that Percy's behavior at Spofford had been good so far, but that St. Michael's didn't want Percy to return. He then asked us who we really were, since neither mother nor aunt was even in the realm of a far-fetched possibility. We couldn't lie any longer.

"We're concerned friends from St. Michael's, and we are willing to try to sway the decision of the home."

Returning to St. M.'s, I spoke with Percy's caseworker, who was strongly against his returning. This attitude was shared by most of the staff supervisors as well. I then resorted to Mr. Johnson, who'd been supportive of Percy once before, to see if, based on his contact with Percy, he would be willing to pass on some encouraging words about Percy to Spofford. He promised he'd try. Percy's future now depended solely on his behavior for the duration of the thirty-day sentence and on whatever support we'd been able to muster through Mr. Johnson and others.

It apparently worked. At the end of thirty days, during which time my own birthday came and I quietly turned eighteen, Percy was allowed to return to St. Michael's. The first thing he did was to come up to the high school group area to let us know that he was back, with one catch: he would have to see a probation officer once a week. That was easier said than done because he didn't care for the probation officer much. I told him that if he didn't go *I* personally would break his neck. Percy smiled and started play-boxing me, testing my strength. I had made a stand. I had gone all out for someone to save him from the unpleasantness of what I had experienced in a lockup facility. My belief in Percy had withstood the test and somewhere deep inside me this helped me see how much I believed in myself as well.

Percy kept on a straight path for about three months, until Christmas time, 1976, by which time I had been moved out of the M.P.U. and re-integrated back onto St. Anne's group. Most of the residents were getting ready to go home to visit their parents or guardians for the holidays. We were in a festive mood, writing "Christmas Daddy" letters. Once in a while, when we wrote these letters to the volunteers who donated items for the residents, we would get lucky and receive something we wanted or needed.

The agency practice was to make a concerted effort to see that every resident is placed somewhere for the holidays, since St. M.'s can be a lonely and depressing place to spend Christmas. That year, I was going to the Harrises. I went for a couple of days and fought with Mrs. Harris, who still constantly chided me. "Why did you have Pete removed from here?," she kept asking. I again cut the visit short and left the day after Christmas. I had a strong feeling that something was going to happen or had already occurred back at St. Michael's with Percy.

I returned to the home that night about 10:30 P.M. About thirty minutes later, one of the male residents came up to the group area to say that Percy and Charlie, another resident who had stayed behind during the holidays, had been picked up for attempted chain-snatching on 42nd Street. Percy had already been issued a juvenile delinquent card. He simply couldn't afford to get into any more trouble with the law and continue to live at St. Michael's. But my hands were tied on this one. He knew the boundaries and knew just how far I would stick my neck out for him. Fortunately, Percy and Charlie were released. No charges were pressed. The two were back at the home by midday of the next day. Percy blamed Charlie for the foolish chain-snatching attempt. I told Percy, "If you get into trouble again, you're on your own!"

Percy *was* arrested again—for breaking and entering—with his brother. This time, the Administration saw to it that Percy was carted off for good. Months later, I learned that Percy had been placed in a juvenile facility called Youth Center Two in the Bronx for eighteen months. After that, I lost track of him. I can only hope that he's alive and well and not that he suffered a predictably sad fate.

CHAPTER 6

COMING OF AGE

Pam continues to make positive strides in all areas. She is relating more appropriately to staff and peers.[24]

My two-year stay at the M.P.U. had drawn to a close. Returning to the main house, where I was assigned to the High School group area for older girls, I took in the increased freedom with enthusiasm. Here I could choose to stay in my own room and refuse to join in the antics of the other residents, which included throwing flour from the third floor down the staircase and so forth. These activities helped some residents pass the time, but I just wasn't interested.

In time, I felt good enough about my privacy to go out and buy plants to brighten up my room. I was able to pay for them with money I had made doing chores and working at Willowbrook through the Youth Corps program. There were eleven girls in the High School group area, each with the privilege of having her own room. Spacious and brightly painted, the rooms faced each other along the length of the hallway. Each girl's room was plainly distinguished by the objects displayed which expressed each girl's individual style.

> Pam is experiencing difficulty adjusting to the High School group primarily because there are several younger residents who are boisterous at night in the group and there is a stealing problem. Pam is becoming involved with other residents' problems. Pam encourages these people to turn to her and then becomes overwhelmed by their problems. Pam is not coming to see the worker and thus the casework process is jeopardized. Pam functions in an aloof, independent fashion. She maintains distance from peers and adults. At times she is extremely manipulative with staff. Conversations with staff in the High School group to prevent manipulation on Pam's part.[25]

In my absence, things had changed at the main house of St. Michael's. As I walked through the various group areas, there was a mood of despair. This was the direct result of events that had occurred in the spring of 1976, six months earlier. The media had been called in by one of the counselors to expose maltreatment of the residents by staff and the waste of food. I knew the counselor who made the call and the intention was not what the media had presented it to be. Their purpose was to show the atrocious living conditions and that no one gave a damn anymore, with the hope that this would lead to improvement. At that time, things had deteriorated so badly that food was often left out overnight or thrown about; boys were being snuck into the girls' quarters to spend the night and vice versa. Worst of all, the counselors who did give a damn about the children were quitting. You never knew from one shift to the next who the newly assigned counselor would be. The stability that was provided by the veteran counselors who knew who you were, what to expect from you and what time to wake you for school or work, was lost, and had been replaced by a hellish confusion.

Our most valued counselors had been the first victims of the widespread attention in the courts that resulted from the television coverage. The camera crew had entered the premises surreptitiously and taken pictures. They had discovered drug and alcohol use—true enough, some of the residents drank and smoked pot and, yes, it was sold on the premises by residents and certain members of the staff. Sometimes residents and trusted staff had smoked pot or drank together. But the only after-effect of the publicity on the already problem-plagued home was that it had become even worse.

As I walked through the halls after my two-year absence, I could hear the kids swearing back and forth at one another and at their counselors. Wanting to see who was keeping up such a ruckus, I tried the door to the St. Theresa group area, only to discover the door was locked. I then ventured off into St. Bernadette's, where girls ranging in age from nine to twelve lived. Glancing at each room in passing, I could distinguish between the children who had been forgotten and those who had not been forgotten by the things they possessed. But this didn't change the fact that we were all in the same boat. When I reached the kitchen area, I came across a new face.

"Hi, who are you?" I asked.

The girl turned around and looked at me with a startled expression. "I'm Jessica, who are you?"

"I'm Pam. I live upstairs. Do you work here?"

"Yes," she answered. But you never would have known it to look at her. She resembled one of the girls she was so small in frame.

I continued to search the kitchen for something to eat, toast or anything, since dinner had been swallowed up by the others before I arrived. Jessica continued to question my presence.

"What are you looking for?" she asked. "Something to eat? Don't you have food upstairs?"

"No. Those pigs ate everything and the main kitchen is closed." Trying to ignore the grumbling of my stomach, I asked Jessica, "How are you getting along with the girls?"

"O.K.," she replied.

"Well I suggest you watch your back because some of them will start shit just to test you—and don't let their boyfriends mistake you for one of the girls."

"I can handle myself," she said. I nodded and left.

Unsuccessful in my hunt for food, I returned to my group area to see if the shifts had changed, hoping I might talk someone into driving me to Pathmark. Nellie was coming on duty and if her car was running, she would take those of us who wanted to go. (Most of the time the van, which had to be shared by the entire resident population, was being used or had broken down.) It was no dice. Nellie was busy with paperwork, tying up loose ends for the investigation by the state's task force. The entire home was in a chaotic state, so my only hope was the 11 to 7 shift.

I had five and a half hours to go. The store was two and a half miles away and I only had enough money for a small steak. I decided I'd see if any of the girls on the floor had a stash of goodies. Finally, I came across Marlene, who had some scooter pies.

"Girl, you don't know what a lifesaver you are. Thanks," I said, grateful that someone had something. "I hope John comes in tonight. He'll take me to the store."

"Why? You didn't get anything to eat either?" asked Marlene.

"No."

"You know, I'm so tired of this. The new counselor acts like she's scared to death of us. She just sits in the counselors' room and reads," she said.

If it hadn't been for hunger, I would never have started her up. My goodness. She was steamed and on and on she went.

"When I came in from work," she said, "I went to take a shower. All the boys were standing in the hall-way and the counselor didn't have the common sense to ask them to leave and I know she saw me go into the bathroom." As I inched toward the door, she said, "O.K. When John comes in, I'll let you know."

Leaving her room, I went down the hall to the kitchen to get some milk to wash down the pies. As I sat there savoring the moment along with the silence, in walked Shera, another resident, one of the oldest in the group. Shera was privileged in her own unique way. She and her sister had been placed in the home at very early ages and could recall when the home was run by nuns. Shera, then twenty-one, still resided at St. Michael's, unlike her sister. When she felt comfort-able with someone she allowed them to visit her room; it was like walking into a thrift shop in the Village: count-less piles of jeans and other clothes neatly stacked in every corner of her room, wherever her dozens of pairs of shoes left space. Shera was a favorite of most of the staff and never seemed to want for anything.

"Hey, Pam, what time is it?" asked Shera, standing in the doorway.

"The clock is right up there. You can see it better than I can, you're standing right in front of it."

"I can't see it," she said.

"Is the clock unplugged?" I asked.

"I don't know, damn it!" She stormed out.

I wondered what her problem was. Millicent, Shera's

tagalong who had witnessed the scene, turned to me and said, "You know, she can't read."

"I'm sorry, I didn't know."

"Well, now she's upset because her social worker just told her that she will have to leave soon because the state won't give her another extension. She's twenty-one and she has to go and she's scared. Shera may have to go into an adult foster care program, so she's got a lot to think about."

All this time, I hadn't known she couldn't read. Then two questions dawned on me: Who's been doing her homework all these years and how is she going to live when she leaves? Shera's experience may be extreme in some ways, but in other ways she was a typical resident. Fortunately for Shera, volunteers who had opened their home to her on weekends also lent a hand at the time of her release. For most residents though, the state is supposed to cut off funding at the age of eighteen, unless you are attending a school of some sort. The rigamarole adds up to a catch-22 since after your release, when you need their support most critically, they drop you like a lead balloon. An individual can request an extension through her social worker, the extensions are usually for six months to a year or they can be granted on a yearly basis, but not to exceed your twenty-first birthday. The problem is that upon discharge most don't have any financial backing or steady income. The state does allot a $500 discharge grant, with one catch, you can't receive this money if you get married or go away to college. Upon leaving, you must go out on your own into an apartment in order to receive the full benefit. And what is $500 to someone faced with the challenge of surviving in the outside world without skills, experience or confidence?

Life in the High School group area continued in a state of continuous upheaval throughout that winter and into the spring of 1977. I knew that soon it would be my turn. One day I received a call from my latest social worker Reha. My nerves were like jelly. Oh, God, I thought to myself, here we go again.

I sat in the waiting area of the Administrative offices watching the phone lines flicker on and off, it seemed that Reha's line stayed busy. Finally, she called me in.

"Hi, Pam. Sit down, I have some news for you."

"Oh?"

"Yes. A Mrs. Goodman called and asked if you would like to babysit for her on Saturday night."

"Well, I guess so," I said.

"O.K., then I'll call you later."

"That's all?"

"Yes."

I left, wondering who this Mrs. Goodman was. I didn't know anyone by that name.

Friday came and still no word. I sat in my room, wondering whether this was another trick. Then I got the call.

"Hi, this is Mrs. Goodman. My husband will pick you up at 5:30."

"Wait. What color is the car and what does your husband look like?" She told me. "O.K., then, good-bye."

Sure enough, he showed up on time. A little apprehensive at first, I got into the car. I didn't talk much but then it was very rare for me to say anything to someone I didn't know. I always wanted to keep my distance. When we reached the house, Jessica came to the door.

"It's you!" I said, as surprised as if I'd seen an angel of God. I'd only seen her once before, the day I arrived back at the main house of St. M.'s. Why me? I wondered.

We ate dinner and afterwards Jessica and I cleared the table. As we did the dishes together, she asked me about my background and how I had wound up in St. Michael's. Never wanting to reflect on the past, I avoided answering the questions as best I could. Then she asked, "How would you like me to be your volunteer?"

I hunched my shoulders as usual and said, "I guess." I couldn't see any reason to refuse. Their house was immaculate, their little girl was cheerful and who could refuse being around a baby? But still I felt I didn't belong in this ready-made family. So what was the problem? I kept mulling this over in my head. I had become leery and retreated into myself for awhile. It wasn't my family. Just the same, here was a stranger who had taken an interest in me. I wondered what she wanted from me—to be her babysitter?

Later, Jessica sat me down and explained that she wanted to give me some place to go when I needed to get away from "the Rock." In time Jessica became my entire support system and was very instrumental in giving me the emotional foundation I needed to go out on my own. God bless her!

The next day I returned to the home. I couldn't wait to tell Cheryl that I too had a volunteer. "It's a secret. No one is supposed to know," I said. This was a precaution that some of us felt we had to take to avoid confrontations with others who might become jealous and in order to protect the volunteering counselor, regardless of whether or not she currently worked at the home. These counselors—who took an interest in us in order to introduce us to a world unlike the one we were living in—were key to our eventual integration into the outside world. Even if it meant sneaking around and not telling certain members of the staff where you were going on weekend passes—especially if your volunteer was also your group counselor—you had to do it. Otherwise, the volunteer could lose her job.

After successfully separating herself from the (M.P.U.) treatment cottage, Pam seems to be establishing a strong relationship with J. G., her sponsor. Visiting: None planned through Social Services. However Pam visits J. G. and S. D. who both reside on S. I. Pam has become belligerent with the worker. She may be struggling with her black identity since it was noted that SICC [Staten Island Community College] has many militant black students and Pam is relating to black counselors and avoiding the worker.

Pam is a neat and clean girl who takes pride in her appearance and her personal belongings. She's recently lost weight and has enhanced her appearance. She has an inflated self-image. She has not yet begun dating and often seems ill-equipped to handle male/female relationships. Pam and the worker have spent several sessions discussing Pam's views on premarital sex. Through the Harris's foster children, she has been exposed to several young girls having babies out of wedlock. She has witnessed their struggles and hardships and feels these are avoidable happenings. She feels that sexual contact is appropriate at certain points in one's development. She is not condemning or moralistic, but rather realistic in her viewpoint. The worker admires Pam's ability to express such deep thoughts.[26]

In May of 1977, I received a phone call from my social worker, Reha. The time had come for me to prepare for my discharge out into the real world from the sheltered world to which I had grown accustomed. I felt confident on the one hand, disillusioned on the other. When I reached her office, Reha was in with her supervisor. "You can go in and wait," I was told.

Before I sat down, I spotted my file on the desk. I opened it, but before I could absorb half a page Reha walked in. I jumped up, startled.

"It's O.K.," said Reha, "It's your file. You want to read it? But before you do, let me tell you something and this is between you and me. Some of the things written in your records don't affect the way I perceive you. Most of what is stated are the slighted opinions of the social workers that have entered your life over the years."

"Well what do they mean by calling me schizophrenic?" I was in tears.

"Pam, it's a crock of shit. There isn't a damn thing wrong with you! Do you hear me? Here's a tissue. Don't let this get in the way of your doing the things you plan to do. You've come a long way. I called you up here to let you know that your discharge grant was finally approved. Sometime next week I'll take you out to look for an apartment. In the meantime, look through the paper for something you can afford."

The following weekend we looked everywhere in areas where, once I got to the location, I knew I would never be able to live. The rents were a bit more than I would be able to afford while continuing school and working during the summer. But I had to do something quick—time was running out! I had only thirty days to go, with no extensions.

In this thirty-day period, life took a turn for the worse. Some madness had circulated around the home about my intentions to deface another resident living in the cottages. Word traveled back to me that the Queen wanted to see me. Now the Queen had earned her nickname by the way she was able to keep her fellow residents in the cottages in deep check. As a bilingual black Hispanic she was adept at communicating with both black and Hispanic ethnic groups. She wanted to see me regarding the Pigeon, an Hispanic girl with a habit of telling lies in both languages. The Pigeon was hoping for a fight but the Queen and I knew one another and, in any case, the Queen was in no condition to do much of anything since she was pregnant. Instead of going up to the cottages, I invited her up to my room. In the meantime, I asked one of the girls to find the Pigeon. "But don't tell her what I want and don't tell her that the Queen is on her way down to the main house," I admonished.

The Pigeon made it upstairs first. When she entered the room, she just stood there. "Yes? What do you want?" she asked.

"Just a minute," I said. Now she was sweating. Then the Queen knocked and came in.

"Pigeon," I said, "did you tell the Queen that I was going to kick her ass?"

"No, but that's what you said."

"When? You're lying!" I shouted.

"Pigeon," said the Queen, "you came to me and told me that, didn't you?"

Then the Queen and I laid into her. Before I knew it,

we had rumbled our way out into the parking lot where, a little worse for wear, she made her getaway.

Forty-eight hours later, a couple of the girls and I were returning from a Kool and the Gang concert at the Garden. Front row seats. We had enjoyed ourselves. It was the last go-round. Quiet, sensitive Cheryl and meek Renee were leaving for the Army and I, the outspoken one, was going out into society. The Three Musketeers were about to separate after three years of living like sisters. We had laughed, cried and sang together and shared a common respect for the substitute mothers in our lives, Bessie and Nellie, the counselors we would have fought to the death for and who held a special place in their hearts for us.

When we stepped off the bus at the ungodly hour of 3:30 A.M., before I could reach the fork in the driveway, I was met by Mark, the grounds supervisor for the 11 to 7 shift.

"Pam, listen, the police are here."

"What?" Just then I knew it was about the Pigeon. "What do you want me to do?"

"Do you have some place to go?" he asked.

I shook my head "No."

"Do you need money? I can tell them you aren't here!"

"No, just leave me alone for awhile. I need time to think. Don't worry, I'm not going to run." That wasn't my style. If I'd done something, then I'd face up to it. I walked around the grounds. By the time I reached the old M.P.U. building, Mark joined up with me again.

"What are you going to do?" he asked.

"I'm going in."

As we walked into the building, he said, "Pam, believe me, I'm sure she deserved it but you could have waited until *I* was on duty to kick her butt! You know, they got the Queen."

"Oh, no!" I said.

> Pam's behavioral problems have come to a head. She was involved with "Pigeon" which resulted in her arrest. Pam appeared in Criminal Court to answer charges of assault. The Criminal Court adjourned in contemplation of dismissal on the assault charges pressed by Pigeon's mother. Pam is on a six-month probationary period.[27]

In the office stood two policemen. I was shaking like a leaf. I was asked to empty my pockets to check for weapons and drugs. Mark had forewarned them that I had been at a concert. Escorted out by the policemen, all sorts of thoughts went through my mind: Would I have to spend the night in jail? Was I going to be thrown out of school because of this?

After they fingerprinted me, I was returned to the home. It was 5:30 A.M., and I didn't want to hear anything from anyone.

Two weeks later, we appeared in court with Reha. I was scared right through because I knew I was of age to go to jail. As the court clerk read off the charges of third degree assault, I thought I'd just die right there. Then the judge asked if we understood the charges. I nodded yes and the Queen yelled out, pointing to the Pigeon, "You'd better keep that bitch away from me!"

I looked at her and elbowed her to shut up, thinking, is she crazy, we'll go to jail! I couldn't believe this had come out of her mouth. The judge was steamed.

"Do you know, young lady, that I'll send you to Rikers?" he said.

"Hum." she grunted.

Luckily, we got off with six months' probation, thanks to Reha who explained that I was about to leave the home and that the Queen was in the process of returning home to have her baby.

> Pam will be discharged to herself in July. We have been preparing for discharge for a year now and she is emotionally and financially ready. Mrs. Wittaker, her maternal aunt, is kept advised of Pam's situation, but is not maintaining contact with Pam or the agency.[28]

The day before my departure, Reha's supervisor, Vasquez, sat me down to offer some words of wisdom. "You are a great manipulator and if you use the skill correctly, you'll go far."

On July 8, 1977, I moved into my first apartment, a small, dimly lit basement rental painted in a very dull brown. Between having to pay my bills on time and keeping up my grades at school, I had my hands full. Then one day I came home to a phone call from Reha.

"Pam," she said, "I've just received a call from the F.B.I."

"What?"

"They were calling about your father. Have you seen or heard from him?"

"No! I don't even know what he looks like. If he walked up to me and slapped me, I wouldn't recognize him."

"I told them that you had no knowledge of where he might be and that you haven't seen him in fourteen years," said Reha.

"What in the devil do they want with him?" I asked.

"I think they said forgery. Also, they wanted to know, if they find him, would you want to see him?"

"No! Do they have my number or address?"

"No, I don't think so. It's O.K., don't worry about it."

The next day, I went off to school. It was a Wednesday and my last class, sociology, let out around noon. When I arrived home, I found a couple in my bed. Apparently, the landlord gave these people entrance to my apartment for their sexual activities. My temper went sky high. I was going to commit murder. I walked around the house cursing like a sailor. At one point, I went to the kitchen drawer to grab a knife. I kept pacing back and forth, trying to think. I couldn't believe this bastard was using *my* apartment so his friends could lay these bitches and cheat on their wives. The lowlifes put their clothes on in a hurry and left. I called Reha at home and she and her husband came over with the police. I kept pondering the fact that I really wanted to kill both the landlord and the bastards I found in my bed. The worst was their story: "We didn't know that anyone lived here. Robert said that the apartment was empty." By the time Reha got there, I was fit to be tied. Reha was crying. She was upset because she knew that if I had been Caucasian, the landlord would never have tried this. Reha's husband kept his cool for as long as he could with the policemen, who claimed that there was nothing they could do. When we calmed down, Reha asked, "What do you want to do?"

"I don't know. I guess I'll be all right," I said, not wanting to be a burden to anyone, but I didn't want to sleep in the bed where those people had been. Also, I had no assurance that the landlord wouldn't just walk in when he felt like it. For all I knew, he could come in and attempt to get revenge by raping me. All sorts of things went through my mind.

Without a home, I went from Jessica's house to Reha's house until I found another apartment, which I didn't care for either. Still on Staten Island, I wound up living below people who were heavily into drugs and I was scared to death of them. My distrust in people grew even stronger.

Then I decided to get off the Island for awhile. I rented a room on Long Island, but that didn't last long either. I became discouraged. The stream of difficulties I'd encountered that summer had taken their toll, although I had found work and also became involved as a volunteer tutoring algebra in the evening to students in the Upward Bound program.

At the end of the summer, I found a day job as a control clerk at a bank. It paid well enough but I still felt shaky. I returned to live with Jessica and her family until I could get back on my feet. Two months later, while I was still living at Jessica's, something interesting happened. I was asked to interview for a second job, part time, as a child care worker on a per diem basis. All of a sudden it hit me that I had come full circle: work in a group home! Me—a counselor! The residents would pulverize me, I decided, but first I had to get through that interview. The interview had taken the form of a challenge. When the moment of truth finally came, I found myself sitting opposite a very familiar face, a former social worker from St. Michael's, someone I liked and who liked me. Where I had feared the worst, the interview turned out to be a piece of cake. I got the job and within thirty days I was living on my own and feeling extremely good about myself.

CHAPTER 7

REFLECTION

Weeks went by without my hearing another word from my prospective new employers. Just when I had begun to wonder whether the position was real or imaginary, I received a call one Friday afternoon asking if I would work the weekend shift in a group home starting that evening. Later that afternoon after leaving my regular day job, with only a couple of hours to change and prepare for the eight-hour shift ahead, I began to feel nervous about my new role as a counselor. But it was too late for second thoughts. All I could do now was take the challenge in hand, fail if I had to, succeed if I possibly could.

The spacious split-level house had once been the home of a doctor. Now it housed six girls of different ethnic backgrounds, ages thirteen to eighteen. The senior child-care worker was on hand to show me around when I arrived. Since it was Friday night, only one of the girls was home, the youngest in the group, Jana. The first thing I noticed about her was her rough attitude. It was what she wanted me to see. But at the same time I could see how unsure of herself she was, how fragile in terms of self-esteem. When asked her name she answered loudly and then rushed suddenly off to her room.

The girls slept two to a room. This made life a little less lonely. It also allowed each girl to positively reinforce her sense of her own identity by decorating her side of the room. But some of the girls, including Jana, left their rooms messy and bare of decorations, which told me they didn't care much for these surroundings.

The senior childcare worker, also called the group mother, gave me the run down of the procedures that had to be followed, such as filling out the log with descriptions of each girl's behavior from the beginning to the end of the shift. Then she wished me luck and left. Before I knew it, it was after 11 P.M. I sat watching T.V., waiting for the others to return. All the while Jana kept her eye on me, passing from the kitchen to her bedroom, to the phone and back again to the kitchen, eating and phoning freely. The girls here were free to live their lives, to make calls, cook and eat, much more than I had been at St. Michael's. The food here was plentiful and was store-bought, not supplied by an institutional service.

Without warning, Jana came into the living room, walked right past me and brazenly changed the channel as though I didn't exist. This behavior was familiar to me.

"Wait a minute," I said, "How do you know I'm not watching this show?"

"Well, then," she shouted, "you don't have to watch nothin'," and turned the set off.

Not wanting to set her off, I left her alone, simply turning the set back on and sitting as I had before. I recognized one of the many tactics used to intimidate new staff. Minutes later, Molly, another resident, strutted in. Her entrance was loud, but curious and she appeared to be good-natured: "Hi, who are you? What's your name?" After I answered her questions, she plopped down on the couch. The remaining girls arrived one by one. By 2:30 A.M. everyone was accounted for. And so ended my first shift, as if I'd done it all a thousand times. Little did anyone know how frightened I had been, or how important a milestone this evening had represented for me.

With time the girls and I got to know each other better. We were able to reach an understanding regarding behavior while I was on duty. Do's and don't's really amounted to nothing more than my respect for their privacy, their respect for mine and our mutual respect for the rules that had been set forth. The girls came to look forward to seeing me on weekends, partly in anticipation of unraveling the mystery I represented to them.

Several weeks after our first encounter, I was promoted to fill the permanent weekend staff position. That night I arrived at the group home an hour earlier than my shift began, weighed down by my heavy bags and the waffle iron I had promised to bring. Now the

girls would have something different for Sunday breakfast. I wanted to make sure to say hello to all the girls
before some of them went out as they usually did for the
evening or on weekend passes. The girls were gathered
in the living room, polishing their nails or primping
themselves for an evening out at the movies. Then one
girl asked me where I lived and whether I knew her
brother who lived at a nearby group home. Soon questions from the other girls were flying from all directions. It didn't take long before they mentioned a name
that was familiar.

"Oh, you know Dorian?" Crystal shouted.

"Yes. She works at another group home," I said.

"Well, she works here now," they all answered.

I got a sense from their responses that they didn't care
for her much.

"How do you know her?" someone asked.

"I was in St. Michael's," I answered.

All heads turned and silence filled the room. I caught
their expressions and burst out laughing. But shock had
set in; there was amazement in their eyes and not even
my laughter could take it away.

"Really! I've heard about that place," one of the girls
offered, breaking the silence. Then Molly asked the
question they all must have had in mind: "Why would
you want to be a counselor?"

The question thrilled me. Why? Maybe I didn't
know the answer myself. Or maybe it had something to
do with turning the stigma that is placed on foster chil-

dren into a mark of hope, a positive alternative. And at the same time perhaps it involved wanting to challenge the system by passing along to the girls my belief that they can get along in the outside world. And it felt good, for once, not to have to hide the fact that I had lived in an adolescent facility myself.

Many people who've lived in facilities as children don't ever put the experience behind them. Not really. Of those that do leave to enter mainstream society, most don't look back, often for fear of being pitied or scorned. Very often they just pretend to forget, as if their personal history were somehow a disgrace—when in fact they should be commended for surviving, for having come so far. But instead of pride, they feel shame. How many times have I run across a familiar face and heard the admonition: Never let on where we've met before in the company of others.

Revealing my secret to the girls made life with them a little eerie. We all shared an experience. With the common bond established, I now felt the time had come to lay down some ground rules. There were certain things that I expected. Cleanliness was essential. I wanted the girls to show respect for themselves and others in the way they presented themselves. And I wanted them to know that however much they enjoyed cursing out other staff members during their tantrums, I refused to be cursed.

During the week between each of my weekend shifts, I maintained regular contact with the house by phone, sometimes speaking with the girls, sometimes with the other counselors. Learning in this way who was going to school, who was doing her chores and who wasn't, I began to get a sense of the girls' individual needs, likes and dislikes.

One Friday night, I came in early. It was spring cleaning time. I wanted to help out, and at the same time to catch them offguard. Earlier in the week I had been told by a co-worker that the girls had been slacking off with their chores. Meanwhile, there was a concert that the girls wanted to see. I had told them that if they could get the agency's permission to go, I would take them. That meant attending school, doing their chores and doing anything else that was expected of them. I couldn't stand a dirty house and I felt that with six girls living here, the place should be presentable at all times. But when I came in that Friday, no one had done anything. And the girls were all clamoring around me wanting to know if I'd gotten the time schedule for the shows.

"No, I haven't gotten anything."

"I asked the group mother about us going to the concert, and she says they won't give us the money," Molly reported.

"And why not?" I asked.

"That bitch won't do anything for us," Molly said.

"Well, I wouldn't either. Look at this place. No one's done their chores and I understand that some of you haven't been going to school. You know that you only have two more weeks to get your acts together."

Mousey looked discouraged. Regardless of what they did, she just knew that certain child care workers weren't going to go for it. I sat them down and told them, "Listen, you get money for recreation, don't you?"

"'Well, yes . . . I don't know," Mousey answered.

"So what are they doing, hoarding the money? Because I know that they have an allotment for recreation?"

"Can you get them to give us the money?" Mousey asked.

"No, I can't. Listen, this is your money. You and the others will have to speak up for yourselves. You're entitled to it and it's there for you."

The next weekend, I arrived to a real surprise. Jana greeted me at the door with open arms. Something's up, I thought. By the time I reached the living room I was ready to collapse from shock. Rosie and her sister had cleaned the windows. Ivy had scrubbed the kitchen until it sparkled. Even Jana had pitched in. I looked up to see her coming down the stairs with all the curtains in a bundle on her way to the washing machine. All I could do was smile. They had definitely touched my heart. "It's clean," I screamed.

"Oh yes. We knew you were coming and we didn't want to hear your mouth," they all shouted together.

We *did* make it to the concert, which they enjoyed so

much they grew hoarse from yelling and singing along. And they kept their promise to get up on time for school the next morning, so they would be able to enjoy more concerts and outings.

Before long a year had passed and several of the girls were nearing their time of discharge, returning home or transferring out. Ivy, the eldest, was preparing for college, hoping to enter the field of health care. Without knowing where they would each end up—who could say?—I felt pride that each of the girls seemed to know she had a choice, each knew that all doors weren't necessarily revolving doors.

But the environment we had been able to create at this particular group home was rare. And even here there were many problems.

Sixteen-year-old Barbara, with her bright and wavy red hair, got along well with the home's black and Hispanic residents. Everybody liked her. No one really noticed that her boyfriend always dropped her off at a distance from the house and never showed his face. Then Barbara was pregnant and it turned out that her boyfriend was her sister's best friend's husband. He and his wife had taken Barbara in when she was a thirteen-year-old run-away. With only the barest education, unable to turn for comfort to either her boyfriend or her sister, Barbara's difficulties were only worsened by the Administration's decision to keep the matter under wraps. Months later she was discharged on welfare with nowhere to turn, a child she couldn't afford, and a social worker whose lack of concern for Barbara's well-being was appalling.

I heard from the other girls that Barbara wasn't doing well and so I took a trip to her new residence. There were unlighted hallways and exposed electrical wiring in the building. In the apartment itself where Barbara and her newborn child were living, there was little food and no heat. Why couldn't they have moved Barbara into a group home for unwed mothers, instead of just pushing her out? Or if they had to send her out, where were the support services she needed? In my anger I was seeing red. But at the same time I couldn't help being impressed by Barbara's courage. The system had failed Barbara, but she hadn't failed. She had bitten the bullet. And eventually she would show she could beat the system. Today, she is a productive working mother. And those of us who may have believed all hope was lost for Barbara have been proven wrong.

Continuing to work as a child care counselor, I was moved to another group home run by a different agency. At the time of my arrival the home was being transformed into a test location, where the agency's administrators were planning to reconstruct a foster family of six natural brothers and sisters. The plan didn't feel right to me from the start. I didn't want to be in on another one of their experiments.

The children had never lived together as a family and now they were being pulled from widely different environments. The worst influences among them seemed to be the strongest, as the younger siblings began to imitate the examples of the oldest. Reports began coming in of thefts and disturbances in the neighborhood and of panhandling as far away as Penn Station. Once the police drove onto the lawn chasing one of the boys. And the more restrictions were placed on the children, the worse they acted. The group home was turned into a living color nightmare. Staff attendance declined. And when staff requested help, the same agency that had proposed the experiment turned stone deaf. Within a year the house was shut down and the children were shifted again.

Here, as elsewhere, the system interfered where they weren't needed and then maintained a hands off policy when they were needed. The result was that these children, among countless others, were emotionally damaged before their lives had begun.

The system is quick to label a child entering the welfare system as emotionally disturbed or maladjusted, and quick to rename that child a ward of the state. But I have questions for anyone who feels comfortable with this state of affairs: How would you react to being removed from your maternal environment and placed in a foster home or institution where you have no real worth and where negative perceptions of the people you were born to are encouraged? How well would you survive the scorn of foster siblings and guardians, or worse, the abuse of alcoholic or psychotic foster parents in whose care you have been entrusted? What effect would it have on you to spend your childhood being shifted from home to home, institution to institution?

Two years after I began writing this book, after winning a court battle to obtain a copy of my records from St. Michael's and other institutions, I received *their* view of most of my thirteen-year stay in the foster care system. It confirmed the accuracy of various complaints I had made to social workers at the time, complaints which were then largely ignored. In the record, caseworkers who believed in me were far outnumbered by those who didn't. I was described as a homicidal psychotic. Both social workers and physicians recommended that I be institutionalized.

The stigma borne by foster care children does not rub off or wear out with time. The pressures on us are different than those familiar to children living in more stable environments. In my own life I have been blessed with a child who is just as bright as I was, yet can claim something I never had: a mother who is sober and stable. This book, which touches on the most intimate and private aspects of my life, embodies both my hope that my own son will never have to travel the same road as I traveled, and my fear for those who still must go that road.

Of the many children who experience the revolving doors of foster care and institutionalized living, few succeed in breaking the cycle. Many of the same children I came to know during my years in St. Michael's were, in the end, unable to adjust. One young woman in particular, Gloria, was among the privileged few then, because she lived in one of St. M.'s group homes, which we considered to be the lap of luxury, as opposed to the dormitories where the rest of us slept. Today Gloria walks the streets panhandling, sleeping in parks, surviving off of trash can scrapings. If it were not for a long time friend who roomed with Gloria during the days of St. M.'s and who today opens her home to feed and clothe Gloria, she would be left to die in the cold. Gloria is unable to accept the world outside of the system that she grew to know too well. She, like many others who have lost their way in society, finds it impossible to be anything other than a victim. Some now watch their lives unfold behind the bars of prison. I have been asked what made me different. Perhaps faith and determination, and a desire to prove all those who accused me wrong. As I live today, my spirit and will, my values and the belief that I can survive, are undiminished.

AFTERWORD

Available data indicates that the United States experienced a decline in the number of children in foster care between the early 1970s and the mid-1980s. In the 1970s, some estimates were as high as 500,000 children; while figures reported in 1985 placed the number of children receiving such care at about 300,000. A recent General Accounting Office study suggests that this reduction may be due in part to the implementation, however incomplete, of the reforms required by the Adoption Assistance and Child Welfare Act of 1980 (Public Law 96 272). This federal legislative action was taken with a view to encouraging states to become more active in monitoring and improving substitute home arrangements for children. Prior to this legislative action, it was thought that too many children were too often shuttled from one temporary home to another; that children were maintained for too long in temporary placements; and that the care and supervision of children in foster care was uneven and inadequate. The G.A.O. study indicates that there may have also been some proportionate reduction in the incidence of these problems. Unfortunately, standards and records in the field are so varied and poor that definitive claims are best not made.

However, what is clear is that, since 1985, there has been a decided increase in the number of children in need of substitute family care. Much of this change in the demand for foster and other kinds of temporary and permanent care for children can be attributed to the increasing number of children victimized by the current epidemic of drug abuse. Even though all of these children have yet to be identified, the U.S. could easily be facing a demand for substitute family care larger than the 500,000 figure of the 1970s. Six-thousand reports of child abuse and neglect were filed during one nine-month period in the District of Columbia; fifty percent involved the illegal use of drugs, and required that the involved children be removed from their homes. In some of our city hospitals, many infants must be treated for drug abuse because they have been born to addicted mothers. Many of these children have no homes to return to upon hospital discharge. We face similar, but more complicated and pathetic circumstances, in the growing epidemic of children victimized by AIDS; whether suffering from the disease themselves, with afflicted parents, or in need of other special care. Add to these numbers children born of teenage, unwed mothers, who are also at risk of growing up in poverty and homelessness. As the nation's economic ability and willingness to provide adequately remunerative work declines, there is no doubt that the groups designated as society's underclass will increase, and that there will likely be increased numbers of children in need of substitute and temporary family care.

So great is this developing need that what the G.A.O. reported as a modest gain in our effort to provide foster and other kinds of temporary care, may now in fact be a severe loss. It is not a simple matter of larger numbers of children requiring care. We are confronted with the older problem of finding suitable placements, preferably in existing families, at a time when some experts believe that there exists a shortage of people willing to share their homes with even "healthy" children. We not only have more children in need, but more children in need of specialized care because of addiction, health problems, and the possible psychological scars resulting from family disruption. We may be faced with the need to return to the system of warehousing children in large institutions unless, as a society, we gain a better understanding of the problems of foster and temporary care, and develop a commitment to finding humane and productive ways to address the present system's failings.

There are at least three categories of problems confronting foster care. The first, and perhaps most pressing, is that of the increasing magnitude and changing nature of the demand for foster care services. We are faced with more children with more complex problems. Furthermore, these children have increasingly come from low economic status, ethnic caste families, making them less attractive to the majority population, even under more optimal circumstances.

The second has to do with the quality of placements made. Here we are faced with the conclusions drawn from conventional wisdom that suggest that smaller in-home or home-like settings are more appropriate, in contrast to the scarcity of such settings, and the pressures to gather children into larger and larger groups. It is this issue, the quality of service, that is the major focus of *Where Is Home?* How long do children stay in temporary placements? We know that many children have as many as five different placements in a three-year period. How do we protect children in foster care from abuse and neglect?

The third set of problems probably speaks best to the second set. These are problems related to management and policy. The Adoption Assistance and Child Welfare Act of 1980 was directed at improving respective states' management of related services. This legislation requires that special attention be given to case planning, to monitoring, to charting the physical and mental health of children in foster care, to reducing the number of placements and the length of time in temporary care, and to the possible return of the child to the biological family. As is so often the case, legislation has proved to be helpful but insufficient. Recall that even without some of the related problems reaching crisis and epidemic proportions, the G.A.O. report indicates only modest gains.

The first and third of these problem categories will require greater governmental and societal effort. It is the second set which cannot be solved at the macro level. Maintenance of foster care quality must be dealt with on an individual level, with those who take these needy children into their homes. A careful and sensitive reading of Pam Jones' story can help us better understand the joys and sorrows, frustrations and rewards, anxieties and strengths, that all of these children experience. Her story also allows us to see what we adults who choose to serve actually do, and fail to do, and how in ways large and small we can make differences in the lives of foster care children. Ms. Jones paints searing and inspiring pictures of the state of foster home care for dependent children, and one person's survival despite the system. For a view of the destructive experience and an appreciation of the determination, effort and faith which enabled one child to mature, this book must be read.

How difficult it must be to determine the meaning of the many events in one's life, and to discern what life is about, without the anchor provided by consistency in some of the people and places which are the central reference points of one's developmental experience. Infants and children are remarkably adaptable. Some seem almost invincible in the presence of circumstances and conditions which appear incompatible with survival, or much less supportive of wholesome development. Yet, it is generally understood that structural consistency (i.e., dependability and regularity in the factors which frame a child's life) is essential to wholesome development. The great tragedy is that so many children do not experience this consistency. The great paradox is that a few manage to survive, and become stable and productive adults.

The study of this paradox has become the focus of an emerging body of social science research. My own studies of those who defy negative predictors of success, people who by all traditional indicators should fail yet go on to succeed, reflect this trend. Pam Jones' story is the account of one such defier. She reflects upon her life as a foster child—subjection to the lack of consistency in people and places in her life, deprivation of a sense of place and belonging, a constant feeling of abandonment, solitude and disconnection. Pam does not address the paradox of survival. Her life illustrates it.

Such a child can emerge whole. Pam's reflections do not answer important questions about defiers or foster care. Her story does not claim to provide solutions. Instead, *Where Is Home?* documents the fact that some do survive with remarkable strength, and serves to remind us that we have major, unresolved problems in the care and protection of children. Furthermore, it indicates that these problems are greatest and most complex in children without able or caring parents, appropriate surrogates, or stable homes.

Provision for the care of children in foster homes is by no means a modern development in human society. When parents were unable, or unavailable, to care for their young in primitive societies, surviving children were usually incorporated into the families of others or into larger social groups. Often the role of the foster child was that of servant, unwanted child, or apprentice. In recent times, under the British and U.S. poor laws, dependent children were placed with families that would support them while teaching them trades. Under such arrangements, the child was expected to work for the person to whom he or she was apprenticed until reaching adulthood. In some rural communities, foster placement was used to provide academic educational opportunities for youths who had outgrown local educational opportunities. These young people were usually supported by their parents, and simply placed with families closer to better schools. Still another pattern prevailed in some Third World nations, where families unable to adequately provide for their young assigned custody to a family friend or otherwise interested person (at times unknown to the parent), who assumed responsibility for the education and support of the child. In this case, the biological parents elected to relinquish their developmental role in the interest of the child's greater opportunity for growth.

During the last thirty years, the foster care of children has come under the supervision of governmental and private child-care agencies. Specific standards exist for foster care. Families and homes are carefully selected. Children, families, and the homes in which they are placed are closely supervised. Foster care families are paid room, board, clothing and a number of incidental child-care costs. In fact, some families find that the care of a small group of foster children can provide sufficient income to permit one of the adults in the home to remain out of the labor force. However, it has not been shown that the availability of remuneration has a negative impact on a family's decision to take one foster child or several into their home. To the contrary, there is evidence to support the assumption that many families add foster care children to their homes out of love for children and a sense of social responsibility.

The most striking changes in foster care have occurred in the nature of the services available to children and families. While earlier concerns may have focused on physical and financial support, more recent concerns have been directed at the availability of both institutional and private home care, one or the other of which may be more appropriate for specific children, and at the total needs of the foster child. Through emphasis on the assessment and care of physical, psychological, and social needs of the children served, active social casework management has become standard procedure.

The best programs take these needs quite seriously and develop placement and intervention plans based upon them. Some of our most able professionals now devote their careers to foster care. Typically, complete case studies are developed on the child, the child's family, and the prospective family prior to a final placement decision. Considerable effort goes into the preparation of all parties. After the child has been placed, the assigned worker is in regular contact with the child and the foster family, in an effort to insure an appropriate match between child and family. The child may be moved to another household if the current placement is inappropriate. This latter protocol can contribute to considerable mobility and cumulative ill effects when the achievement of such a match is elusive.

In general, modern programs of foster care can be said to be humane, child-centered and enlightened in intent. For many children the system works quite well, and is associated with high degrees of satisfaction and even praise on the part of many participants and observers. There is no question that the effort is directed towards the best interests of the children and families served. Nevertheless, when the system does not work and there are too many instances of failure—the costs in failed children and frustrated and disrupted receiving families are enormous. We do not have good indicators of successful and unsuccessful outcomes of foster care. Large numbers of people who are the products of foster care arrangements will testify to the important role this care played in their lives. There are also sizeable numbers of individuals ready to report details of abuse and frustration. Public attention is often called to these errors, mistakes and failures. So much so that, as Pam Jones points out, considerable negative stigma is attached to one's identity as a product of foster care. But what alternatives exist in the face of increasing numbers of dysfunctional families with children in need of surrogate providers?

Perhaps more than any other species, humans are essentially social beings. We are born virtually incapable of providing for our own physical care. We have too few of the instinctive traits which inform the organized behavior of lower forms of animal life, therefore making it necessary that we learn most of our organized purposeful behavior. Consequently, we are dependent upon social interaction for our initial physical survival, and ultimately for our social and psychological existence. It is this social dependency that makes the human family so essential to the survival and subsequent development of infants and children. The family should provide initial physical care and the earliest socialization experiences. One's family is usually the primary source of personal identity. It is only when the primary family fails, or the child has grown older, that extra-familial and surrogate sources become important; and even then much extra-familial influence is mediated through the imprints made by that initial experience of family.

One never seems to be emancipated from this essential social dependence, even interdependence, since the human social need is not simply to receive but to give—to exchange. The social nature of humans thus complicates the problems of care for dependent children. They cannot be left to provide for themselves. They cannot simply be placed on the public dole. We have learned that children cared for in institutions must be organized into small groups that permit, and even encourage, more intimate and personal interaction. Even in untutored societies, dependent children without families are placed in families for care and supervision until they are able to care for themselves. In societies in social chaos, such as those devastated by war, where large numbers of children are left homeless and without families, the children come together in groups, with the older and more experienced providing leadership and care for the less mature. The social nature of human beings seems to require that our children be cared for in families or family-like groups.

It is in response to the social nature of human beings, and the functional necessity for family-like groups for the nurturing of the young, that substitutions for family care have been developed. Such arrangements continue, and will do so, because the human condition requires their existence. It is to be remembered, in light of failures and abuses, that foster care arrangements serve important and essential social purposes. If foster care did not exist, all societies would find ways to invent it.

One hopes that foster care services can be improved, that abuses can be avoided, and that failures can be prevented. In many, and perhaps most, such programs we have moved toward this achievement. But as long as there are unwanted children, and dysfunctional families, there will be foster care programs in which some children and some families will not develop successfully. Unfortunately, colloquial judgment has it that there are too many that do not succeed and, as some of us would add, too few people who care sufficiently.

The complexities of modern life make it increasingly difficult for traditional nurturers, such as family, schools, or religious establishments, to supervise the socialization and protection of our children. As public awareness, and possibly the magnitude, of the problem has increased, the availability of good institutional and foster home placements for dependent children has not kept pace. But even more problematic is the fact that the same forces exacerbating the demand may also be contributing to a decline in the quality and quantity of substitute families and facilities. In the face of rampant social pathology, we experience a reduction in our confidence in the integrity and stability of the people, families and institutions who might provide substitute care and protection.

Pam Jones' story reminds us that when adults are troubled, children in their care will likely suffer. This is common even in biological families. The response to personal or social stress by substitute parents, and their interaction with children for whom they are responsible, is often more troublesome. What can be done about this problem, by a society that considers itself humane, is the challenge raised by *Where Is Home?* More than just an examination of the foster care system is required.

Meaningful solutions need to be found by examining the ways in which parental competence can be strengthened, and by improving the economic and social conditions required to promote competent child care. There are no problems more pressing than those encountered by children without able and caring parents, or appropriate surrogates and stable homes in which to be loved and nurtured.

—EDMUND GORDON
JOHN M. MUSSER PROFESSOR
OF PSYCHOLOGY
YALE UNIVERSITY
FEBRUARY 1990

NOTES

[1] St. Michael's Placement Summary—p. 1, 9/21/73

[2] Euphrasian Residence Record—p. 2, 8/14/73

[3] Euphrasian Residence—p. 2, 8/14/73

[4] Euphrasian Residence—p. 2, 8/14/73

[5] Euphrasian Residence—p. 2, 8/14/73

[6] Euphrasian Residence—p. 1, 8/14/73

[7] St. Michael's Placement Summary—p. 2, 9/21/73

[8] St. Michael's Record Sheet—pp. 1, 2, 6, 9/24/73

[9] St. Michael's Record Sheet—pp. 6, 7, 10/16/73

[10] St. Michael's Record Sheet—p. 1, 10/73

[11] St. Michael's Record Sheet—p. 2, 10/9/73

[12] St. Michael's Record Sheet—p. 2, 1/8/74

[13] St. Michael's Summary p. 2, part 5, 3/19/74; Record Sheet p. 2—3/74

[14] St. Michael's Record Sheet—p. 7, 10/73

[15] St. Michael's Record Sheet—p. 13, 3/74; p. 16, 7/74

[16] St. Michael's Record Sheet—p. 16, 7/74

[17] St. Michael's Record Sheet—p. 18, 10/74

[18] St. Michael's Record Sheet—p. 24, 9/75

[19] St. Michael's Record Sheet—p. 20, 1/75 and p. 22, 5/75

[20] St. Michael's Record Sheet—pp. 21, 22, 4/75

[21] St. Michael's Record Sheet—pp. 24, 28, 27, 32, 5/76

[22]St. Michael's Record Sheet—p. 33, 9/76
[23]St. Michael's Record Sheet—p. 37, 1/77
[24]St. Michael's Record Sheet—p. 37, 1/77; p. 37, 3/77
[25]St. Michael's Record Sheet—p. 29, 1/77
[26]St. Michael's Record Sheet—p. 38, 4/77
[27]St. Michael's Record Sheet—p. 38, 4/77–5/77
[28]St. Michael's Record Sheet—p. 2, 5/77